OXFORD
THEN & NOW
FROM THE HENRY TAUNT COLLECTION

MALCOLM GRAHAM & LAURENCE WATERS

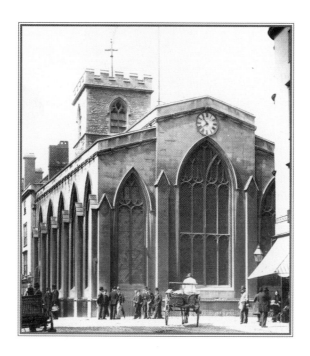

SUTTON PUBLISHING

Oxfordshire Books

Sutton Publishing Limited
Phoenix Mill · Thrupp · Stroud
Gloucestershire · GL5 2BU

First published 2006

Copyright © Malcolm Graham and
Laurence Waters, 2006

Title page photograph: The Horspath village
carrier passes idlers at Carfax, 1890.

British Library Cataloguing in Publication Data
A catalogue record for this book is available from the
British Library.

ISBN 0-7509-4224-X

Typeset in 10.5/13.5 Photina.
Typesetting and origination by
Sutton Publishing Limited.
Printed and bound in England by
J.H. Haynes & Co. Ltd, Sparkford.

 Oxfordshire Books

Picture Credits

Most of the Henry Taunt photographs in this book are reproduced by permission
from the extensive Oxfordshire County Council collections held by the Oxfordshire
Studies service in Oxford Central Library. The authors are also most grateful to
the following for kind permission to reproduce the following: National Monuments
Record Centre, English Heritage: 89 top left, 90 top, 105 top; The President and
Fellows of Magdalen College, Oxford: 42 bottom.

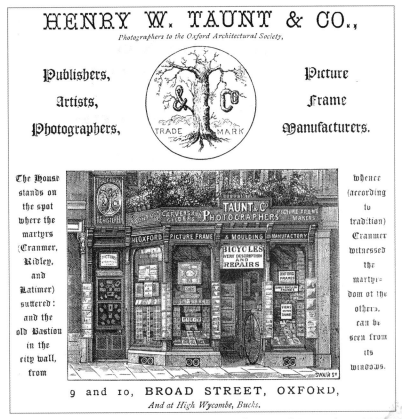

Advert for Henry Taunt's business, showing his Broad Street shop, 1878.

CONTENTS

Henry Taunt in 1880 when he was standing for election as a city councillor.

Taunt's shop at 33 Cornmarket Street,
c. 1874. The window is characteristically
filled with examples of his photographs and
picture frames.

Henry Taunt's shop and studio at 9–10 Broad
Street in the 1880s, with two women watching
road-menders from an upstairs window.

INTRODUCTION

Henry Taunt, the veteran Oxford photographer, commented in 1918 that 'All photographs have some limited historical interest; those taken today will many of them be much wanted in fifty years.' The value of his work was already appreciated during his lifetime: in 1910 D.P. Watkins, the manager of the Church Army Press, had expressed the opinion that Taunt's works were 'a memorial to and of yourself which will stand forever'. The *Oxford Chronicle* remarked in 1911 that because of his work, future Oxonians 'will have no difficulty in conjuring up the city as it is in the second decade of the Twentieth Century'.

When Taunt died in 1922, however, there was a real danger that his photographs would simply be lost, as were most of those taken by his long-standing Oxford rivals, Hills & Saunders, Gillman & Co. and James Soame. Outside the major cities the infrastructure for preserving material of local interest was rudimentary and there was as yet little appreciation of the value of images as historical source materials. Clearance work had already begun when the local historian Harry Paintin, who had used Taunt's images in published newspaper articles,

encouraged Ernest Skuce, the city librarian, to purchase the collection. Between 1924 and 1925 the City Library acquired a large quantity of negatives, prints, papers and manuscript folders for a total of £98 10s. This comparatively modest investment has had incalculable benefits as Taunt's work has continued to inform and delight successive generations.

Penson's Gardens, St Ebbe's, *c.* 1912, with two small boys standing outside Taunt's birthplace and childhood home.

Taunt was born in Penson's Gardens, St Ebbe's, Oxford, on 14 June 1842. His father, also Henry, was a plumber and glazier from Bletchington, and his mother, Martha, was a domestic servant from West Ilsley, Berkshire. Taunt himself later described them as 'poor but respectable and respected parents'. Like so many others at the time, they probably came to Oxford in search of work. Their small two-storey house was in an area that had grown rapidly since the 1810s to house a wave of incomers like themselves.

The young Henry Taunt, who was an only child, was educated at St Ebbe's National School and Sunday school and also at the church school in his mother's home village. His recollections suggest that he was an inquisitive lad, avidly exploring his surroundings and regularly taking a boat down Trill Mill Stream (an open sewer) in order to avoid paying a toll at Folly Bridge lock. He quickly asserted his independence, continuing to play with the sons of Timmy Bricknell, a drunken old bricklayer, against his parents' wishes: the boys were older and introduced him to 'no end of tricks'.

After leaving school in about 1852 Taunt worked with his father for a time and then became a shop boy at several High Street shops. He stayed two years at Charles Richards'

Henry Taunt and an assistant on the River Thames at Old Ham Weir below Lechlade, *c.* 1860. Taunt's portable darkroom can be seen on the river bank behind them.

bookshop and auction room, demonstrating there his insatiable thirst for knowledge by reading books during 'the vacation when things were very leisurely'. In 1856 he made the crucial decision to cross the road to 26 High Street, joining Edward Bracher, an early Oxford photographer, as a general utility hand. His first jobs included polishing silver plates for daguerreotypes and showing 'Dons and Laity and Ladies and Gentlemen of every class . . . up those squeaking stairs' to the roof-top gallery where their portraits could be taken in daylight. He took his first photograph, a group in Exeter College quad, in about 1858, and some of his earliest surviving photographs of Oxford and the River Thames were taken soon afterwards.

His first major Thames expedition was at Christmas 1859 when he rowed up to Lechlade and returned when the river was in flood, narrowly avoiding death or serious injury as he rushed beneath the bridge at Hart's Weir. This adventure led on to almost annual river trips, whether by camping gig in his young days or by horse-drawn houseboat later in life. When, in 1863, increasing competition and other commercial interests encouraged Bracher to sell his business to the High Street stationers, Wheeler & Day, Taunt became their photographic manager.

Taunt set up as a photographer on his own account in 1868, opening his first shop in St John's Road, now St Bernard's Road. He then operated from premises at his home at 67 George Street before moving to a small but central shop at 33 Cornmarket Street in 1869. His photographs of the Oxford area and the River Thames soon attracted praise and he demonstrated his flair for publicity in June 1870 by displaying in his shop window a photograph of the Head of the River procession of boats that he had taken only a few hours earlier; a passing reporter duly filed a piece for the *Standard*, noting the excellence of the image and the interest it had generated. Taunt also publicised his work through magic lantern lectures from 1871 and his first book, *A New Map of the River Thames* (1872), included paste-down prints of his photographs as well as his own survey of the river between Oxford and London. In the early 1870s he had a separate shop selling window glass in Friars Entry; this was perhaps associated with his picture framing work. By 1874 he had to move to larger premises at 9 and 10 Broad Street and he opened a branch at Easton Street, High Wycombe, which flourished between about 1875 and 1889. Taunt travelled extensively by bicycle and put his knowledge of machines and local roads to profitable use by selling and repairing bicycles at his Broad Street shop and at a separate depot near the Oxford Union in New Inn Hall Street, the modern St Michael's Street, between 1878 and 1882.

A catalogue issued by Taunt in about 1874 indicates that he had already taken over 3,000 photographs, which could be purchased in five different series at prices ranging from 6d to 3s 6d. Many of these images were of well-known Oxford scenes for the university market and for visitors to the city but others illustrated the River Thames, churches, mansions and towns around Oxford and the River Avon. The new Broad Street shop had a photographic gallery upstairs for portrait work and Taunt also advised potential customers that the firm was always ready to photograph 'Gentlemen's Seats, Churches, Interiors, Groups &c. Attendance with Camera. Distance unimportant.' A dispute in 1884 resulted from one such journey to Upper Heyford when the client refused to pay for Taunt's blurred photograph of his prize sheep. Taunt took him to court and won the case by arguing that the sheep would not keep still.

The pressing need for more space must have encouraged Taunt to lease Canterbury House in Cowley Road in 1889. He renamed the house Rivera after the River Thames and established his main photographic and printing works in the extensive grounds. Taunt continued to live in Broad Street, and when the census enumerator caught up with him in 1891 he listed no fewer than thirteen occupations – artist in water colours, photographer, author, designer, lecturer, lantern-slide maker, picture frame-maker, gold blocker and printer, publisher, mount-cutter, ornamental card-maker, entertainer and gilder.

His versatility and energy did not save him from financial trouble in 1895 when a dispute over renewal of the lease of his Broad Street shop forced him into bankruptcy with debts which he estimated at over £3,000. He moved his central premises to 41 High Street and later to No. 34, but from 1906 he operated solely from Rivera and customers were advised that the house was five minutes' walk beyond the horse-tram terminus at Magdalen Road beside a large aspen tree. If anything, Taunt became more active in these later years, seizing upon the craze for picture postcards to produce his own series and becoming a prolific author of local histories and guidebooks, publishing over thirty titles himself; he also diversified into quality printing and even produced his own newsletter, *Notes and News from Oxford's Famous City*, for a time. Photographic work continued apace but Taunt's assistants, notably Randolph Adams, who was with him from the 1880s, took many of the later photographs. In 1914 Taunt enhanced his photographic coverage of north Berkshire by purchasing 1,300 images from the estate of Frederick Ault, a Stanford in the Vale photographer. The First World War provided some new commercial opportunities in the form of greetings cards for loved ones at the Front, calendars and patriotic songs, but Taunt was left with few employees and the business never recaptured its pre-war dynamism. Taunt died at Rivera on 4 November 1922, having assembled a collection of over 60,000 photographs in sixty years, and he was buried at Rose Hill Cemetery five days later.

Taunt was a tall man and he cultivated a full beard which gave him a distinguished appearance. He almost always wore a reefer jacket and yachting cap as though he was just leaving for another voyage along his beloved River Thames. William Adams, the son of Taunt's long-serving assistant, saw both sides of the photographer's character: 'He could talk to you like a father, he could be a real dear old chap and he could play merry blazes!' Taunt was also a competent musician and one-time organist at St Mary Magdalen Church, and he demonstrated a sense of fun by writing humorous poetic jingles and giving annual children's entertainments and magic lantern shows, which caused great hilarity. On the other hand, he positively revelled in arguments, and in 1876, for example, he successfully prosecuted a cart driver who had obstructed his bicycle on the Radley Road near Abingdon. In 1922 he lambasted a railway official: 'please don't write childish twaddle but do your own business properly if you can, and wait until I ask you before you attempt to teach me how to manage mine'. He never suffered fools gladly and in 1878 was fined for assaulting his apprentice, James Best, after the latter had spoiled some plates and refused to take out the firm's heavy quadricycle for a third day running. In the ensuing struggle, oil, water and glass were used as weapons before Taunt grabbed Best by the throat and pushed him out of a window; not surprisingly, Best's apprenticeship was later cancelled because of the poor treatment he had received.

As an Oxford businessman and citizen, Taunt was a spirited and regular campaigner on local issues. He battled for clean city water in 1880, when he threatened to photograph the pond life that consumers received with their unfiltered supply, and in 1906 he strongly opposed, on economic grounds, the proposal for electric tramways; five years later he was raising environmental fears about tram wires in Oxford's High Street. He was incensed by a high stile which the City Council erected in 1897 at the entrance to the Cowley Road recreation ground opposite Rivera. Taunt wrote to the council, reporting that 'the broad top rail is utilised by young Roughs in the day time as a vantage point on which to sit and slang their mates and the passers by and at night it is used for purposes which are usually done in dark corners . . .'; when his letters achieved nothing, he threatened to go out and saw the stile down. In terms of national politics, Taunt was a Conservative, but he was very much against local party politics, arguing that it had no place in 'the matter of carrying on our City Business, sweeping the streets, keeping up the roads, looking after the safety of people and their dwellings, collecting the Rates and spending the Ratepayers' money'. He stood unsuccessfully as an Independent candidate for the City Council's West Ward in 1880 and 1881, and supported Fred Valters, a Ratepayers' Association candidate, for East Ward in 1907.

Taunt and two assistants with a picnic beside their camping gig, *c.* 1878.

Taunt and a lady, possibly Fanny Miles, relax on his horse-drawn houseboat, 1895. The boat provided a comfortable base for Taunt's later trips down the Thames and the roof was an excellent vantage point for views of regattas.

Taunt married Miriam Jeffrey, an Oxford dressmaker, on 17 September 1863, but the couple had no children. He clearly had a roving eye and relationships with other women, and in 1883 a court order made him pay 5s a week towards the maintenance of the illegitimate child of Louisa Bricknell of Isis House. He is said to have fathered other children – one by Eliza Wheeler, an employee; and an illegitimacy case linking him with Emily Bowell of Cowley was withdrawn in 1891. Perhaps his most enigmatic relationship was with Frances or Fanny Miles who managed his High Wycombe branch from the 1870s and lived at Rivera from 1889. Taunt claimed at the time of his bankruptcy that 'I had lost everything, and nearly myself, except honour and my "Little Lady"', his pet name for Fanny Miles. Taunt and his wife moved into Rivera with Fanny Miles in 1906 and William Adams, a young employee, gained the impression that Miss Miles was the 'governor's lady'. After Taunt died, without leaving a will, it seems to have been Fanny Miles and not his wife Miriam who determined the fate of his estate.

Randolph Adams, Taunt's former assistant, kept the postcard business going for a time after 1922, but Frank Organ, the Oxford builder, purchased Rivera and began to clear the premises. The City Library came to the rescue, but having taken in all the material, staff faced the impossible problem of housing it in a building condemned as inadequate back in 1911. Some negatives were judged to be of little value and disposed of for use as greenhouse glass; from 1940 most of the remainder was gradually transferred to the National Buildings Record, now the National Monuments Record Centre in Swindon. The prints remained in Oxford and are some of the finest images in the photographic collections held by Oxfordshire County Council's Oxfordshire Studies service. More Taunt prints than negatives survived and full public access to his photographs was hampered for many years by the division of the collection. Support from the New Opportunities Fund enabled English Heritage and Oxfordshire County Council to scan the 14,000 surviving Taunt images between 2001 and 2003, virtually reuniting the collection and making it available on their respective websites.

Henry Taunt's photographs range well beyond the confines of Oxfordshire and cover the whole length of the River Thames from source to sea. Oxford and the immediate environs of the city remained the main focus of his work, however, and this book emphasises the local importance of his legacy by comparing and contrasting his images with views of the same

Some of Taunt's employees in the firm's handicraft room behind Rivera, *c.* 1910.

scenes taken by Laurence Waters between 2004 and 2005. The book consists of a series of journeys, and the first two are effectively armchair walking tours exploring the heart of Oxford then and now. **City Centre West**, the first journey, begins at Carfax and takes in the western side of the city centre; **City Centre East** begins at Magdalen Bridge and covers the main university area. Then come four wider-ranging journeys, still well within the range of Taunt's quadricycle, which take the reader to points north, east, south and west of the city. The section **North from St Giles'** extends out to Yarnton, Cassington and Kidlington. **East from St Clement's** goes out through Headington to Forest Hill and Wheatley and returns via Horspath and Shotover to Cowley. **South from New Hinksey** heads off through South Hinksey to Kennington and returns through Littlemore and Iffley. **West from Park End Street** takes in Botley and North Hinksey on the way to Cumnor and Besselsleigh. A final section **By River & Canal** is a virtual voyage, following Taunt's gig or houseboat on a course from King's Weir in Wolvercote to the King's Arms at Sandford-on-Thames.

As the *Oxford Chronicle* anticipated nearly a century ago, Taunt's work does have an almost magical ability to conjure up the city and district as it was in his time. Some scenes have scarcely changed, externally at least, in the eighty or more years since he or one of his assistants photographed them; others, for good or ill, are barely recognisable. As a photographer, Taunt was a consummate professional and it was said that he could 'make such unpromising subjects as gasometers and waterworks look picturesque'. His photographs would therefore have been a valuable record even if he had done nothing beyond his commercial work. In fact, photography was a key part of Taunt's life and the images that reflect his many and varied interests raise the value of his work way above that of most contemporaries. His photographs provide a fascinating window on the past and form a lasting memorial to a most remarkable Oxonian.

1

City Centre West

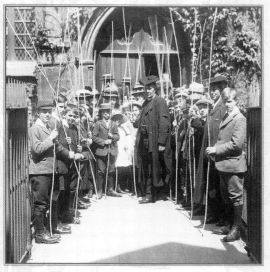 

Left: Beaters of the bounds of St Michael at Northgate's parish boundary outside the church, 1914. They were setting off with their willow wands to continue the ancient Ascension Day custom of beating the parish boundaries. The practice, which originated long before detailed mapping, ensured that local people would always be aware of the boundaries in the event of any dispute.

Right: Today's beaters of the bounds leave St Michael's Church. The tradition continues in central Oxford but following the amalgamation of parishes the route differs, having to take account of major redevelopments. One stopping place guaranteed to startle shoppers is a boundary marker on the ground floor of Marks & Spencer's Queen Street store.

Carfax and St Martin's Church with John Harris, the Horspath village carrier, turning right into Cornmarket Street, 1890. St Martin's Church was first recorded in 1004 and became the City Church, attended regularly by the mayor and corporation. The medieval and later structure was demolished and rebuilt in 1819–21, leaving only the fourteenth-century tower.

St Martin's Church was demolished again in 1896 to widen the road at Carfax; the tower was retained and converted into a clock tower the following year. The HSBC bank to the right of the tower was originally Frank East's store, designed by Henry Hare and built in 1900. Lloyds Bank on the extreme right was designed in flamboyant style by Stephen Salter and built in 1900–1.

Cornmarket Street, looking south towards Carfax, 1907. Victorian commercial developments, most notably the three-gabled façade of Grimbly Hughes' high-class grocery store (1864), dwarfed the seventeenth-century timber-framed building housing Twining's grocery shop. Boffin's half-timbered restaurant at Carfax closes the view with Boots the Chemist next door representing the arrival of national chain stores.

Pedestrians have enjoyed the freedom of Cornmarket Street since buses were removed in 1999. Barclays Bank expanded across the site of Twining's old premises in 1923, surprisingly echoing the design of the adjoining Victorian building. Littlewoods bought Grimbly Hughes' store in 1960 and replaced it with the utilitarian structure which is now a McDonald's restaurant. At Carfax, Marygold House replaced Boffin's in 1930–1 as part of the contemporary redevelopment of the area.

Cornmarket Street, looking north towards the Anglo-Saxon tower of St Michael at the Northgate Church, 1885. Zacharias & Co., an outdoor clothing business best known for its 'Wet-Off' coats, occupied part of a former fourteenth-century inn opposite, with Harvey's the tea blenders on the corner of Ship Street. Tramlines were laid in the centre of the street when horse trams were introduced to Oxford in 1881.

The historic character of Cornmarket Street is still evident at this end. A tree partially obscures the church tower but the former Zacharias' premises were carefully reconstructed after the closure of that old Oxford business in 1983. On the left-hand side of the street, tall bay-windowed frontages dating from the late eighteenth century mask older timber-framed buildings.

Looking into Magdalen Street from Cornmarket Street, 1907. This is a deceptively quiet scene, showing uncrowded pavements and a single horse-drawn carriage waiting at the roadside. The contemporary rapid expansion of Elliston & Cavell's department store beyond George Street told a more prosperous story, and the Northgate Tavern nearest the camera had been another recent development, built in 1879.

Change of use is the main theme here, with many of the buildings from 1907 still surviving. The Northgate Tavern building survived closure in 1971, and despite a huge redevelopment scheme between 1999 and 2000 Debenhams kept the old Victorian and Edwardian frontages of Elliston's. The NatWest Bank, the former George Hotel on the corner of George Street, was added in 1912, when it was described as 'Oxford's first skyscraper'.

St Aldate's from Carfax, showing the Town Hall of 1751–2 and, further down the street, Tom Tower, 1893. A police constable is on duty at the entrance to Queen Street and a shop blind is down at Wyatt's the drapers to protect the stock from the afternoon sun. Electric street-lighting had just been introduced at Carfax and the wooden lamppost was an embarrassing stop-gap measure because imported ornamental lamp-standards had been slow to arrive.

Tom Tower still forms the backdrop to a quite different scene. A new and much larger Town Hall designed by Henry Hare was built between 1893 and 1895, while the southern corners of Carfax were set back and rebuilt in a chaste neo-Georgian style in 1930–1. Traffic lights were installed at Carfax by the mid-1930s but the tradition of a 'Carfax Copper' stationed in the area was to last another forty years.

Blue Boar Street from St Aldate's, 1900. This seventeenth-century and later timber-framed building, once the Unicorn Inn, contrasts with the exuberance of the Town Hall to the left. Steps behind the two little boys lead up into the purpose-built City Library which had operated from one room beneath the old Town Hall since its opening in 1854.

A woman using an umbrella as a sunshade passes the little-altered premises of Mathews Comfort. The shortcomings of the new City Library were soon exposed and the building was condemned as inadequate by 1911. The library remained, however, until 1973 when it moved at last to new premises in the Westgate Centre. Two years later the Museum of Oxford, telling the history of the city, opened in the old library premises.

Christ Church from St Aldate's, with a milkman and his handcart in the foreground, 1890. The St Aldate's front of Christ Church was begun by Thomas Wolsey in the 1520s as part of his new Cardinal College, but it remained unfinished at his death in 1529. Work resumed in the 1660s and was only completed in 1681–2 when Tom Tower, designed by Sir Christopher Wren, was built above the entrance.

The St Aldate's front of Christ Church was largely re-faced in the 1960s and the formerly soot-blackened Georgian house on the extreme left has also now been cleaned and restored. There is generally less traffic in St Aldate's than there was before the introduction of the Oxford Transport Strategy in 1999 and the line of bus shelters bears witness to the number of local bus services.

Tom Quad at Christ Church, *c.* 1876. The temporary belfry or 'tea chest' of 1872 shown here became a target for the wit of Charles Dodgson, then a tutor at Christ Church. Clean stonework is evidence of recent building work and the addition of battlements around the quad and pinnacles on the hall has just begun.

Scaffolding on Christ Church Cathedral tower marks the continuing struggle to maintain Oxford's historic buildings. The battlements and pinnacles were completed in the later 1870s and the sumptuous bell tower, designed by Bodley & Garner, replaced the belfry before 1876 and 1879. The same architects were also responsible for the vaulting around Tom Quad, suggesting the cloister which Wolsey had envisaged. The statue of Mercury in the centre of the quad was added in 1928.

St Aldate's, looking north towards Christ Church from the Waterman's Arms, 1900. In medieval times development had extended beyond the town walls and down St Aldate's, and by the seventeenth century houses filled the street frontage and much of the land behind it. The brick-built Apollo pub on the left, near the man with a pony and trap, was an isolated example of rebuilding in 1861 and the area remained seriously overcrowded.

The former Apollo in the foreground and Tom Tower provide continuity in a street that lost most of its houses and its population to slum clearance between the 1920s and the 1960s. Macmillan House behind the trees on the right filled a gap in the 1980s, and the stone-fronted police station beside the bus shelter was built in 1938. This section of St Aldate's, part of the main A34 until the 1960s, is now at times uncannily quiet.

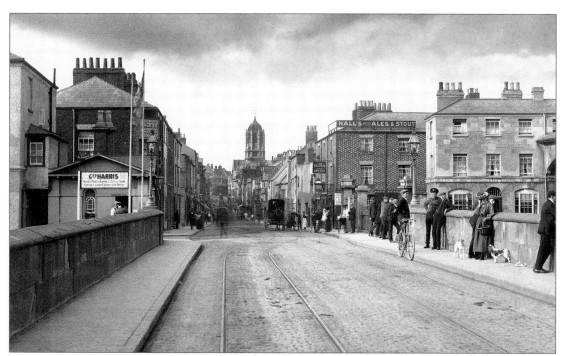

Looking up St Aldate's from Folly Bridge, 1907. The rebuilding of Folly Bridge in the 1820s helped to reshape this end of St Aldate's. The punt-hire premises on the left were built as a toll-house in 1844, the Dolphin & Anchor pub on the right with its chequered brickwork dated from around 1830 and the imposing stone house beside it, occupied at this time by Salter Bros, was part of a wharf built in 1827.

The tramlines disappeared when buses replaced Oxford's horse trams in 1914, but the bridge parapets are unchanged and Salter's premises, threatened for a time with demolition, were triumphantly restored as the Head of the River pub in 1977. Away to the left, Folly Bridge Court provided flats in the 1980s in the style of riverside warehouses, replacing the former 1830s houses.

Charles Street, St Ebbe's, looking west towards Pensons Gardens, 1912. Taunt thought that the building on the left, on the corner of Wood Street, was part of the medieval Blackfriars and that the gabled houses on the right dated back to the seventeenth and eighteenth centuries. Other houses were part of the early nineteenth-century development that quickly transformed St Ebbe's into a populous suburb.

Redevelopment in the 1950s and '60s wiped out virtually all of St Ebbe's, and so residents were relocated to new estates on the outskirts of the city. The Oxford Preservation Trust acquired and restored the gabled houses on the right in 1971. Charles Street was given back its old name, Turn Again Lane, in 1972 and the council houses on the left were built in the 1980s in a vernacular style.

Church Street, St Ebbe's, looking west towards Paradise Street, 1907. Most older properties in the former Pennyfarthing Street had been cleared for larger three-storey houses during the nineteenth century, a prominent exception being the very low two-storey building on the right. The half-timbered building also on the right was the former Britannia pub, much altered by Harry Drinkwater in 1878.

All the properties in Church Street were demolished in the late 1960s to make way for the Westgate Centre: only this stub of the street, renamed Pennyfarthing Place, remains. The building now occupied by the G Bar opened in 1973 as the Pennyfarthing pub. A path to the left leads to Sainsbury's, a large store when it opened in 1973, and Westgate.

St Ebbe's Church and the entrance to Church Street, 1907. The church, with a rare dedication to a seventh-century Northumbrian saint, was first recorded in 1005, but the growth of the parish in the 1810s made necessary this new building, designed by William Fisher and built in 1816. St Ebbe's Street became a bustling shopping centre in Victorian times and included Cape's drapery business on the right.

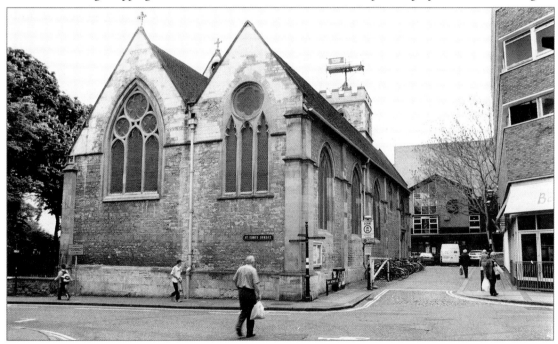

St Ebbe's Church is little changed but Cape's, the store where Oxonians could buy almost anything, closed its doors for the last time on 13 January 1972. The Victorian premises were soon torn down and replaced by a smart new Fenwicks fashion store; Bar Med has been the most recent occupant of the building.

The parish of St Ebbe's seen from the church tower in 1908, showing the slate roofs and chimneys of the closely packed terraced houses built between 1810 and 1840 – in 1901 the parish was home to almost 4,500 people. Circus Yard in the foreground provided premises for Witham's Tripe Dressing Factory and carriers' carts parked there on market days.

The huge Westgate multi-storey car park, opened in 1974, accommodates the vehicles that have taken the place of carriers' carts. To the right of the parked cars there is a glimpse of Tennyson Lodge in Paradise Square, a 1990s development on the site of the Victorian St Ebbe's School. Two distant masts pick out the Oxford Ice Rink, designed by Nicholas Grimshaw & Partners and opened in 1984.

St Ebbe's Street, looking north towards Queen Street, 1907. Cape's premises, acquired or newly built in the 1880s and 1890s, are prominent on the left and demonstrate the success of the business established in about 1877 by Faithful Cape, a Lancashire man. The Royal Blenheim pub on the right was built in 1897, luring day-time drinkers by its ornate style and using the ornamental lantern at night to attract them like moths to the flame.

The Royal Blenheim still attracts attention, albeit with a smaller lantern, on the corner of St Ebbe's Street and Pembroke Street. Towards Queen Street, Ramsay House rears up beyond older properties. In 1997–8 it was part of a development that provided a BHS store and City Council offices on the site of City Chambers, a 1960s office block.

Queen Street, looking towards Carfax and the distant spire of All Saints' Church, 1907. The three-gabled Queen's restaurant, dating back to the seventeenth century, now looked almost out of place in a shopping street dominated by Victorian commercial buildings such as the Wilberforce Hotel (1888) on the left. Horse trams linked Oxford's suburbs with the city centre but this was a golden age for cycling shoppers.

Queen Street was closed to most traffic as long ago as 1969 but pedestrians still have to beware of the many buses that use it. Morris Garages brought down the Queen's restaurant, replacing it in 1912 with the gabled and half-timbered building now occupied by Evans and Maxwell's. This was the firm's first purpose-built car showroom, providing display space on two floors; it remained in use until larger new premises were opened in St Aldate's in 1932.

Queen Street decorated with patriotic flags during Queen Victoria's Diamond Jubilee, 1897. Pedestrians spill out into the street to enjoy the decorations festooning shops such as Badcock's, Jackson's and Prior's on the left. Beyond the Wilberforce Hotel on the right, the four-storey stone building formed the frontage for Hyde's clothing factory, a major employer of women and girls in Victorian Oxford.

The façade of the Wilberforce Hotel was retained in a redevelopment scheme in the 1980s, but Hyde's frontage was shorn of most of its detail back in the 1960s. Since the early 1970s the Westgate Centre has terminated the view at the end of Queen Street, replacing what local people knew as Macfisheries Corner.

Above: New Inn Hall Street, looking north towards George Street, 1880. The gable end on the left was a relic of the medieval New Inn Hall, the buildings of which had become the Royal Mint during the Civil War. Hannington Hall, next door, had been built on part of the site in 1832. The Wesley Memorial Church, with its prominent spire, was designed by George Bell and was completed in 1878.

Left: A new central girls' school, partly visible on the left, was built next to Hannington Hall in 1901. Both buildings are now part of St Peter's College, founded as St Peter's Hall in 1929. The scene is otherwise little changed except that a 1930s neo-Georgian building now closes the view, not the George Street Congregational Church built in 1832.

Beaters of the bounds of St Michael at the Northgate parish in the playground of the City of Oxford High School for Boys behind George Street, 1914. The group is posing in front of a cut-down section of the medieval city wall above which Elm Cottages had been built in the early nineteenth century. The first house in the row stood on an old defensive bastion.

The beaters no longer come to a spot where the city wall maintains continuity between then and now. Elm Cottages were demolished as slums in the 1930s and Wesley Memorial church hall took over part of the site. The Matthews Building of St Peter's College, completed in 1971, rises from the city wall on the right. The City of Oxford High School for Boys left George Street in 1966 and the university's Classics Centre now occupies the buildings, using the former playground as a garden.

Demolition of old properties on the corner of George Street and Victoria Place, 1886. George Street was outside the city wall and house building here was at its height in the seventeenth century. The raised footway at this point was formed in 1667 and the buildings behind it must have been erected soon afterwards.

Oxford's first New Theatre was built on this site in 1886, taking advantage of the university's relaxation of a ban on the staging of plays during term time! A second New Theatre was needed after a fire in 1908 and the present building, designed by W. & F.R. Milburn, is the third one, erected in 1933–4. The city's largest theatre accommodating over 1,800 people, it was known between 1981 and 2003 as the Apollo but is now the New Theatre once more.

George Street from Hythe Bridge Street, 1920. Advertisements hide the frontages of early nineteenth-century corner properties, seeking to catch the eye of travellers approaching from the railway stations. Along George Street, the roofline of Lucas's clothing factory, built in 1892, is prominent on the right; further on, the ornamental turret marks the City of Oxford High School for Boys, which opened in 1881.

The High School building, now the university's Classics Centre, is visible in the distance but the foreground is very different, the product of redevelopment in two stages. The right-hand corner was rebuilt in about 1930 while the tall, highly ornamented offices on the left were part of the Gloucester Green development designed by Kendrick Associates and built between 1987 and 1989.

St George's Tower from Quaking Bridge, 1901. The tower is usually dated to around 1074, soon after the establishment of Oxford Castle in 1071, but it may have originated as a slightly earlier watch-tower protecting the western entrance to the town. There was a castle mill at the foot of the tower by 1086 and the name Quaking Bridge, referring perhaps to a drawbridge, was first recorded in 1297.

The vegetation conceals the loss of the castle mill, sadly demolished for road widening in 1930. St George's Tower has been restored to allow public access as part of the Castle redevelopment. Beyond the current Quaking Bridge, which dates from 1835, St George's Gate was built in 1995 to provide student housing for St Peter's College.

Lower Fisher Row, looking north towards Pacey's Bridge in Park End Street, 1920. Fisher Row, home to generations of Oxford watermen and fishermen, was built on the bank between two branches of the River Thames, the Castle Mill Stream seen here, and the Wareham Stream behind these houses. Park End Street was a new road, which sliced through the row in 1769–70.

Pacey's Bridge was rebuilt in 1923 as part of a larger scheme to improve the western exit from the city. The flood-prone houses in Fisher Row were later condemned and most of them were pulled down in 1954. The site became a quiet public garden, but on the left, the completion in 2005 of new apartments called the Stream Edge transformed the area once more.

Upper Fisher Row from Hythe Bridge, 1885. The hythe or wharf on the Castle Mill Stream served river traffic from the upper Thames, and unloaded produce could quickly be carted into central Oxford. Since the area was known as Thieving Corner in the eighteenth century, security must have been a continuing problem. Most of the houses seen here dated from the seventeenth century, with a few at the far end added in the nineteenth century.

In the early 1920s two pairs of council houses replaced the picturesque but unsanitary old properties. Upper Fisher Row is now fenced off from the Castle Mill Stream and the separation is reinforced by trees and shrubs. In the foreground, the Oxford canal towpath is home to many waterside plants now that it is no longer kept free of vegetation.

The medieval south range of Worcester College, 1880. These buildings date from the fifteenth century and were part of Gloucester College, founded in 1283 to enable Benedictine monks to study at Oxford. After the Dissolution of the Monasteries by Henry VIII, Gloucester Hall took over the site and saved these buildings by continuing to use them.

A garden sprinkler waters the beautifully tended lawn in front of the south range. The exterior has scarcely changed and varied plants and climbers add to its picturesque character.

Lounging undergraduates in the arcade beneath Worcester College Library, 1885. Gloucester College was refounded as Worcester College in 1714 and Dr George Clark soon prepared plans for a complete rebuilding. The front building, comprising library, hall and chapel, was built soon after 1720 and a new north range in 1753–9, but the full scheme was never completed.

Today's undergraduates hurry through the same arcade. The major change is a poignant one, the memorial on the wall outside the hall recording the names of ninety-two members of the college who died in the Second World War.

Beaumont Street, looking west towards Worcester College, 1919. St John's College had Beaumont Street laid out in 1822 as part of a plan to develop college land north of Gloucester Green. Three-storey terraced houses fronted with ashlar stone filled the street within a decade, bringing a touch of Bath or Cheltenham to Oxford. The Ashmolean Museum, partly visible on the right, was added in 1841.

In smoke-free modern Oxford, Beaumont Street's stonework looks much cleaner but the road is now a busy thoroughfare and traffic has become the current concern. The extension west of the Ashmolean Museum was a sympathetic addition to the scene in 1939–41 and, on the left, the Randolph Hotel extension of 1952 imitated the Gothic style of the original Victorian building.

Looking north along Walton Street, 1919. The seventeenth-century stone cottages behind the safety chains on the left show how much the original street level has been raised over the years. Beyond those houses, Ruskin College was built in 1913 to give working men the opportunity of an Oxford education. Three-storey terraced houses occupied the right-hand side of the street in two phases, beginning in the 1850s and the 1870s.

Parked cars have replaced the odd tradesman's cart and some of the safety chains on the far pavement are broken, but the view has changed remarkably little.

2

City Centre East

Left: A man and two small children pose outside J.H. Darwood's Italian warehouse in St Mary's Entry, *c.* 1885. The lane leads towards High Street with the chancel of St Mary the Virgin on the left and timber-framed buildings dating back to the seventeenth century on the right. On the opposite side of High Street Nos 102–3 were occupied at this time by Spiers & Son, a well-known fancy goods business. *Right:* Pedestrians head towards High Street past buildings adapted for Brasenose College. Spiers went out of business in 1889 but their former premises are little changed. A pavement of stone setts and a Victorian gas lamp, now converted to electricity, add interest to the modern scene.

Central Oxford from Magdalen Tower, *c.* 1897 – an almost magical townscape that had evolved over many centuries. On the left Thomas Graham Jackson's neo-Jacobean Examination Schools had been completed in 1883. The Radcliffe Camera, built in 1737–49, and the fourteenth-century spire of St Mary the Virgin are prominent features on the skyline. New College tower, dating from 1396, can be seen away to the right behind the low thirteenth-century tower of St Peter in the East.

High Street no longer slumbers in the afternoon sun but this special view of Oxford's towers and spires has scarcely changed. The Examination Schools are now partly obscured by the Eastgate Hotel of 1899–1900 and, to the north of High Street, St Edmund Hall added a residential block in 1968–70 which has a conspicuous six-gabled roof.

Donkey-power and horse-power on Magdalen Bridge, *c.* 1885. Magdalen Tower dominates the view as it has done since it was built for the recently founded Magdalen College between 1492 and 1509. The bridge was rebuilt in the 1770s to designs by John Gwynn but growing traffic and horse trams led to sensitive widening in 1883–4. Taunt has obscured the tram lines here, probably for aesthetic reasons.

Magdalen Bridge today, equipped with cycle lanes and relieved of some of the traffic that once dominated it. Magdalen Tower was refaced in the 1980s and is now an almost luminous feature at the end of the bridge. Magdalen Bridge itself has needed public appeals in recent times to renew the balusters, restore the parapets and lay stone paving.

The Eastgate Hotel at the corner of High Street and Merton Street, 1897. The east gate in Oxford's medieval town walls guarded the entrance to High Street at this point. The gate was finally cleared away in 1772 as part of a contemporary drive to modernise the city and widen its streets. The Eastgate Hotel building was probably erected soon afterwards and by 1840 had become a public house, the Flying Horse.

A new Eastgate Hotel designed by E.P. Warren was built in 1899–1900 and extended much further down Merton Street than its predecessor. A cartouche on the High Street frontage at first-floor level shows the former, eighteenth-century East Gate. Adjoining eighteenth- and nineteenth-century properties in High Street have been retained, but the brick façade of nos 69–70 was rendered in 1935.

Looking west along High Street from Queen's Lane, 1885. A man pushing a hand-cart is taking advantage of the better road surface between the tram tracks in an otherwise peaceful street. Hansom cabs are waiting outside Queen's College which dominates High Street at this point with its classical front built between 1734 and 1760.

As the High Street has been closed during the day to most traffic except buses since 1999, it is probably now easier to appreciate the splendour of High Street than at any time since the early 1920s. The gabled High Street elevation of the Durham Building, built in 1903 for University College, is the only notable architectural change, just visible beyond the bus on the left. Buses have taken over from hansom cabs outside Queen's College.

Encaenia procession outside Queen's College, 1897. Visitors and passers-by stop to watch the procession of people, led by university officials, who were on their way to the Sheldonian Theatre to receive honorary degrees. Traffic, including a horse tram, trundles past regardless, and some of the spectators seem more interested in the photographer on his step-ladder.

The architectural fabric is virtually the same but the modern view has buses outside Queen's College and cyclists accounting for most of the moving traffic. The prominent sign in the foreground warns drivers of unauthorised vehicles to turn round and find another route through the city centre.

A college gardener stands poised with his mower in the Front Quad of University College, *c.* 1875. The quad was built in stages between 1634 and 1677 and the statue of James II in a niche in the gate-tower was a final touch in 1687. The three-storey quad was built of local Headington stone which had clearly decayed by this time, requiring the replacement of battlements and parapets.

A busy moment in Front Quad where the condition of the buildings with renewed stonework now matches that of the well-kept lawns.

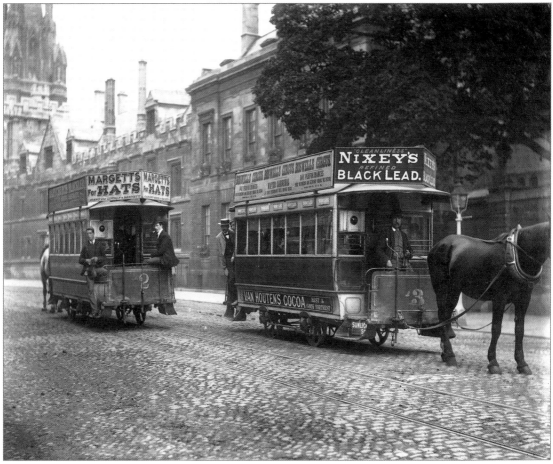

Horse trams outside All Souls' College in High Street, *c.* 1890. When horse trams were introduced into Oxford in 1881 people complained that they would ruin High Street, and the tram company had to minimise disruptive noise outside the Examination Schools by laying wood blocks between the rails. This picture of single-decker trams in a historic setting shows that their impact was in fact quite negligible.

Public transport in the same place today as a taxi and an Oxford Bus Company No. 5 bus for Blackbird Leys pass through the bus gate outside All Souls'. The sycamore planted in the eighteenth century still overhangs the college wall at this point. Behind the functional but unappealing traffic management measures, the Warden's Lodgings of 1704–6 and the adjoining Victorian Gothic range have both benefited from recent restoration.

High Street, looking west from St Mary's Entry towards Carfax, 1885. Standen's tailoring business occupied 31 High Street on the corner and the Principal of Brasenose College had his lodgings in the eighteenth-century house next door. Taunt had joined Edward Bracher's photographer's studio at No. 26 in 1856 and he crossed the road to Wheeler & Day's as their photographic manager in 1863.

Brasenose College had long nursed the ambition to build on the High Street frontage, and this range, designed by T.G. Jackson, achieved that objective in two stages between 1887 and 1911. Nos 24 to 31 High Street were demolished, leaving just a few town houses on this side of the road between St Mary the Virgin's and All Saints'. The tree overhanging the pavement on the right is one of the street's contemporary delights, producing a mass of pink almond blossom in spring.

The Radcliffe Camera from the south-east, 1865. This striking circular library was built with money left to the university by John Radcliffe (1652–1714), Fellow of Lincoln College and court physician to William III and Queen Anne. It took many years to acquire the site and select an architect and the Camera, designed by James Gibbs, was not completed until 1749.

Both the Radcliffe Camera and the Bodleian Library further along Catte Street have emerged from a soot-stained past and are now in pristine condition. Iron railings around the Camera, installed in 1836 to deter undesirable folk from sheltering in the once open loggia under the building, were removed as unfashionable in 1936. Picnickers sprawling outside this most delightful of libraries have led to the return of railings which were instantly adopted for secure cycle parking.

The Old Quad at Brasenose College, *c.* 1875. The quad was begun in 1509 with the battlemented hall on the south side and the gate-tower of 1512 to the east. Dormer windows in the roof mark the addition of a third storey in the early seventeenth century. The large statue, a replica of Giovanni Bologna's *Samson Killing the Philistines*, was installed in the quad in 1727.

Old Quad in a meticulous state today with stonework restored and the grass mown in regular stripes. The statue is missing, the victim of undergraduate vandalism in February 1883 when Brasenose College went Head of the River during the Torpids races and celebrating students smeared it with paint after lighting a gigantic bonfire in the quad.

Brasenose College and Radcliffe Square, 1875. The sixteenth-century front of Brasenose College is visible beyond the spreading branches of a fine horse chestnut tree, Heber's Tree, in Exeter College Fellows' Garden. The tree was so called because it shaded the Brasenose College rooms of Reginald Heber (1783–1826), later Bishop of Calcutta. Before railings were erected around the Camera, a group of drunken dons from Brasenose are said to have spent a night going round and round the building trying to find their way back.

The recent loss of the horse chestnut tree profoundly affected this corner of Radcliffe Square. Brasenose College, with newly restored battlements, is much more evident and the entrance to Brasenose Lane can be seen beside the high wall to Exeter College Fellows' Garden. The cobbled and paved street surface complements the many architectural delights of the square.

The south-east corner of Old Quad in Hertford College, *c*. 1880. Hertford College was refounded in 1874, inheriting these seventeenth- and eighteenth-century buildings from Hart Hall and Magdalen Hall. The top floor of the building on the left was a nineteenth-century addition for Magdalen Hall, which had moved to this site from Magdalen College in 1822.

T.G. Jackson's chapel erected in 1908 now abuts the remaining eighteenth-century house. The tall chapel with a polygonal north-west tower almost obscures Hawksmoor's twin towers in the nearby North Quad of All Souls' College.

New College Lane from Catte Street, 1880. The New College bell-tower in the background was erected in 1396 and was the first documented building in Oxford to be built of limestone from the local Headington quarries. Hertford College, founded in 1874, had recently taken over the buildings of Magdalen Hall to the right of New College Lane, which had been erected in 1820–2.

Hertford College's 'Bridge of Sighs', designed by T.G. Jackson and built in 1913–14, now hides the New College bell tower. The bridge provides a link between Old Quad and the Jackson-designed North Quad which was built between 1900 and 1931. The beer delivery beyond the bridge is for the Turf Tavern, tucked away down St Helen's Passage on the left.

Demolition for Hertford College's North Quad exposes the remains of the Chapel of Our Lady in Catte Street, 1902. The octagonal chapel was built in 1521 next to the Smith Gate in Oxford's city wall. The building was later converted to secular use and was sometimes incorrectly described as Oxford's oldest house. Aware of the chapel's true significance, T.G. Jackson, the college architect, decided to incorporate it into the new quad.

The New College Lane frontage of Jackson's North Quad now obscures the chapel which was largely rebuilt to form the Hertford College Junior Common Room. On the opposite side of Catte Street, the Clarendon Building was designed by Nicholas Hawksmoor in 1711–13 to house the Oxford University Press.

A quiet corner of New College Lane, 1908. The view shows the property of four colleges, including Queen's College stabling on the left and the New College boundary wall on the right. Beyond an ancient rubble stone wall, the Codrington Library of All Souls' College, completed in 1720, stands to the left of the newly built Hertford College chapel, designed by T.G. Jackson.

A pedestrian corners at speed in a view changed most obviously perhaps by the effects of stone cleaning and the introduction of yellow lines. New Provost's Lodgings for Queen's College in 1958–9 led to alterations on the left and New College added to the height of their boundary wall to deter intruders, possibly after the wartime removal of iron railings.

The Turf Tavern in St Helen's Passage, 1908. The pub had its present name by 1847 but its buildings date back to the seventeenth century and it was known originally as the Spotted Cow. St Helen's Passage is a polite modern rendering of the old name Hell Passage, which probably derived from a disreputable gambling house in this out-of-the-way spot.

The Turf survives as one of Oxford's favourite pubs, its tiny low-ceilinged bars being supplemented by outdoor seating areas in the garden to the left in the shadow of the thirteenth-century city wall.

Two men watch from a first-floor window at 36 Holywell Street, c. 1900. This fine timber-framed building, dated 1626 on one of the decorative corbels at eaves level, was part of the contemporary development of housing on the Merton College estate in Holywell Manor. The well-known Oxford building firm Knowles & Son, established in 1797, had offices and a yard here from 1870.

No. 36 Holywell Street, like the adjoining properties, is beautifully maintained and the only external changes have been the installation of shutters and the addition, or restoration, of a few small windows. Knowles & Son moved to a new yard in Osney Mead in 1966 and vacated its offices here ten years later. The Holywell Music Room, away to the right, has lost its iron gates and railings.

Holywell Street, looking east towards Park Passage and the distant Magdalen Grove, 1900. A woman pushes her bicycle past the arched gateway to Charles Symonds' livery stables, a business much frequented by Victorian undergraduates, including the fictional Verdant Green. The street was an attractive mixture of seventeenth- and eighteenth-century properties adorned here and there by window boxes and sun blinds.

Careful developments behind the street frontage have left the physical fabric of Holywell Street little changed, which, since the banning of through traffic from 1975, has reverted to being a peaceful backwater. The sycamore tree billowing into the street adds character to the scene.

A corner of New College, showing a postern gate in the thirteenth-century city wall, 1901. William of Wykeham, Bishop of Winchester, acquired the site of New College in 1379, three decades after the area had been depopulated by the Black Death. The town was struggling to maintain the walls in these circumstances and granted him this part of the inner wall on condition that the college would look after it in perpetuity.

New College employees inside the gateway that now protects a staff car park and an area of wheelie bins. Ivy has been stripped from the ancient walls, allowing careful restoration of the stonework and a glimpse of the Robinson Tower built in 1896. The City resumed regular inspections of the walls in 1962 and the Lord Mayor and accompanying councillors still make a ceremonial visit every three years.

Staircase IX and the rear elevation of the south range of Wadham College, *c.* 1870. Founded in 1610 by Nicholas and Dorothy Wadham, wealthy Somerset landowners, the college was substantially complete by 1613. The five-bay stone building known as Staircase IX, which fronts on to Parks Road, was built as accommodation for undergraduates in 1693. Here their Victorian successors are watching the photographer from its wide-open windows.

Luxuriant vegetation masks the south range and permits only glimpses of the refaced Staircase IX building. An arched gateway to the left leads out into Parks Road near the King's Arms.

Trinity College and Broad Street from Taunt's shop at Nos 9 and 10, late 1880s. Behind the ornate seventeenth-century gate and contemporary cottages, Trinity College was experiencing a period of expansion with the building of the north and east ranges of Front Quad to designs by T.G. Jackson. Broad Street became a cabstand in the later nineteenth century and well-wishers subscribed to the wooden shelter in 1885, providing cabbies with a refuge from the weather between fares.

The same view today with pedestrians taking advantage of the fact that traffic in Broad Street is now heavily restricted. The centre of the street became a car park in 1928 and some parking continues, pending a decision on the future of this wonderful urban space. The façades of Trinity Cottages were retained in the 1960s when they were rebuilt for college use. The rearing bulk of the New Bodleian Library away to the right represented more drastic change between 1938 and 1940.

The Garden Quad at Trinity College, *c.* 1900. Sir Thomas Pope refounded Trinity College on the site of Durham College in 1555 and Garden Quad was built in three stages between 1668 and 1728. The garden was originally laid out with avenues of pleached lime trees and an elaborate maze, but this formality gave way to grass in the nineteenth century, providing space for archery and croquet.

The stripes in the lawn are more pronounced and the stonework of the unassuming Garden Quad has been restored. The rear elevation of Durham Quad on the left was originally part of Durham College and was built in 1417–21; the dormer windows were added in 1602.

Dons outside the New Hall at Balliol College, 1886. Balliol grew both in size and reputation during the Victorian era and the New Hall, designed by Alfred Waterhouse, was built in 1876–7 to replace the small fifteenth-century hall in the Front Quad. Staircase XXII, partly visible to the left, was built at the same time to provide extra accommodation.

One mature tree largely hides Waterhouse's Hall and another obscures the Bulkeley-Johnson Building to its left. The latter was designed by Geoffrey Beard of Oxford Architects Partnership and built on the site of Staircase XXII in 1968.

Broad Street, looking east past Balliol College, 1904. The Master's Lodgings on the left and the Balliol front beyond were designed by Alfred Waterhouse and built in 1867, replacing Georgian buildings. Exeter College, beyond Turl Street, had also changed the face of Broad Street with a new range built between 1833 and 1856. The ornate but poorly sited street lamp had recently brought electric light to the street for the first time.

Tall lamp-standards in a neo-Victorian style now sit uneasily on one side of Broad Street. Before and during the Second World War the City Council was planning to redevelop old properties west of Turl Street but nothing came of these schemes. The major alteration to the street scene has therefore been the Thomas Wood Building of Exeter College of *c.* 1964, a plain ashlar stone structure on the far corner of Turl Street.

The Front Quad of Lincoln College, 1914. This photograph was taken during the beating of the parish boundaries and shows boys involved in the ceremony grappling with a rather uncomfortable reward, heated pennies thrown from upper windows of the quad. The now ivy-covered quad was built in the fifteenth century, with the later addition of sash windows and battlements.

The Front Quad today with creeper still more rampant. The only revealed piece of stonework is a carving of the Lincoln Imp over a doorway beside the hall in the north-east corner of the quad.

Turl Street and Lincoln College from the corner of Brasenose Lane, *c.* 1870. Lincoln College was founded in 1427 and the Turl Street frontage dates from the fifteenth century, although it was considerably remodelled in the eighteenth century and then Gothicised in 1824. A gigantic horse-chestnut tree billows across the cobbled street from the college stables and an early street-nameplate, dating perhaps from the 1840s, announces Brasenose Lane.

Lincoln College has profoundly influenced this scene, not least by the recent refacing of its Turl Street façade. In 1938–9 the college replaced the chestnut tree on the corner of Market Street with Lincoln House, a neo-Georgian development. It had a small library built at the end of the street in 1906 and then between 1971 and 1975 converted the redundant All Saints' Church into a sumptuous library. Bicycles now rule the roost in Turl Street and other traffic is restricted south of Market Street.

Ducker & Son's shopfront at 6 Turl Street, 1911. It was established here in 1898 and flourished with the development of Varsity sport, supplying specialist boots and shoes for rugby, soccer, cricket and rowing, as well as bespoke footwear for wealthy undergraduates. German air ace Baron von Richthofen was one of the firm's early customers.

Ducker's still flourishes at No. 6 and only minor changes have been made to the shopfront. A modest hanging sign seeks to attract the attention of the approaching passer-by.

The western end of High Street, looking towards Carfax from Turl Street, 1907. Carfax Tower, rather than St Martin's Church, now terminates the view, and cyclists, tramlines and a tall electric lamp-standard have introduced a touch of modernity to the busy street scene. Prominent older buildings include the Mitre Inn, with an eighteenth-century and later façade, on the corner of Turl Street and the Georgian frontage to the covered market, built in 1773.

The view looks almost unchanged, even down to the lamppost on the corner of Turl Street. The differences here are only obvious to long-term residents who remember the Mitre as a hotel rather than as a restaurant and recall former High Street shops like Webber's, the International Stores, Sainsbury's and Russell Acott's.

Payne & Son's shopfront at 131 High Street, 1911. Payne's were established as silversmiths and jewellers in Wallingford in 1790 and occupied these eighteenth-century premises in 1888. The carved mastiff holding a clock was an unusual advertising feature, attracting customers to the shop. A fishmonger's open-fronted display occupied No. 130 to the left and a chemist's shop was then at No. 132.

Payne's and the firm's mastiff provide continuity in the High Street, as does the Chequers pub down the adjoining alleyway which retains features from about 1500. A branch of White Stuff now occupies the former fishmonger's and No. 132 is a building society office. Planning guidelines now prohibit the kind of bold commercial advertising that once filled blank spaces on Nos 131 and 132.

Left: Swan Court off High Street, *c.* 1870. The Swan on the Hoop inn to the right of this courtyard was first recorded in 1397 and the distant buildings on the High Street probably dated from the thirteenth century. The backland properties on the left were built before 1682 at a time when the rising population of Oxford was leading to much infill development.

Below: King Edward Street, a commercial development by Oriel College, replaced Swan Court and adjacent High Street properties in 1872. John Ruskin, who became Slade Professor of Fine Arts in 1870, is reported to have recoiled with horror when he first saw these plain yellow brick buildings through the builders' hoardings.

Above: Blue Boar Street, looking east towards Bear Lane, 1900. Three- and four-storey houses built in *c.* 1800 bask in sunshine that streams across the Christ Church boundary wall. Part of Peckwater Quad, designed by Henry Aldrich, Dean of Christ Church, and built in 1705–14, is visible in the distance, and there is a glimpse of the Oxford University gymnasium (1859) on the corner of Alfred Street.

Right: Demolition of properties on the left widened the road and created a seating area for the Bear Inn further along. The pub took the name of a former coaching inn in High Street and before 1801 was known as the Jolly Trooper; it is famous today for its collection of ties. Peckwater Quad has been refaced with new stone and the Blue Boar Quad, designed by Powell & Moya and built in 1968, oversails the boundary wall on the right. The former gymnasium is now occupied by offices.

Corpus Christi College and Merton College Chapel from Oriel Square, 1890. Richard Foxe, Bishop of Winchester, purchased the site of Corpus Christi College from Merton College in 1513 and the college buildings were occupied by 1517. The blackened north front seen here and the decayed portion of Oriel College to the left bear witness to the effects of air pollution on porous Headington stone.

Substantial restoration work has preserved all these historic buildings into the twenty-first century and the only major addition to the scene is the gabled Thomas Building below Merton College Chapel; erected for Corpus Christi College as recently as 1927–9, it fits unobtrusively into the townscape. The modern bracketed street-light makes a positive contribution to this remarkable view.

The Fellows' Building at Corpus Christi College, *c.* 1865. A college gardener poses with his lawnmower outside the classical-style building built between 1706 and 1712. William Butterfield's three-storey Grove Building, erected for Merton College in 1864, is visible in the background.

The crumbling south façade of the Fellows' Building was restored in the 1950s, making it a lovely backdrop to the sunny garden in the foreground. Spreading branches now mask the Grove Building which Merton dons found too prominent for their taste, having the top storey removed in 1930.

Christ Church Meadow Buildings from the Broad Walk, 1880. Thomas Deane designed the Meadow Buildings in a Venetian Gothic style. Erected between 1862 and 1866, the buildings provided fifty-one sets of rooms. The Broad Walk was laid out in the 1660s by Dr John Fell, Dean of Christ Church, and elm trees, two of them seen here, were planted along its length in the eighteenth century.

The Meadow Buildings today, showing the results of recent restoration to chimneys and dormer windows. Dutch elm disease destroyed the avenue o trees along the Broad Walk in the 1970s, giving walkers round Christ Church Meadow more expansive views of Oxford's historic buildings.

Sunlight and shadow in Mob Quad at Merton College, 1890. Merton College was one of Oxford's first colleges, founded in 1264, and Mob Quad – the origin of the name is unknown – was the first complete quadrangle built between 1304 and 1378, setting a pattern for later foundations to follow. The building with a higher roof line in the corner of the quad was the college treasury. Dormer windows were added in the seventeenth century, lighting new rooms in the roof space.

Mob Quad is now in a much finer condition and all its chimneys have been removed as coal fires are no longer needed to keep the rooms warm in winter. The roof of the late thirteenth-century choir of Merton College Chapel is visible in the background.

Dead Man's Walk in Merton Field, 1907. There are a number of explanations for the name of this path below the old city wall, one being that Jewish burial processions came this way in medieval times on the way to the Jews' burial ground on the site of the Botanic Gardens. Another is that the name referred irreverently to the number of old men who enjoyed taking this sunny walk.

The seat beside the bastion has vanished, discouraging gossip here and perhaps removing a source of distraction for Merton College fellows in their garden above and behind the city wall. Vegetation has been removed from the old wall but shrubs are softening the appearance of the Merton Field fence.

The cobbles of Merton Street lead the eye towards Magdalen College tower, 1907. The building on the left was part of T.G. Jackson's Examination Schools development of 1876–82. Beyond it, a group of three-storey houses dating from the seventeenth and eighteenth centuries contrast harmoniously with mature trees spilling over the rubble stone wall that marked the boundary of Merton College Fellows' Garden.

New Warden's Lodgings for Merton College were built on the bend in Merton Street in 1966, obscuring a fine view. Merton Street has a few car-parking spaces beside the college boundary wall, but even when Oxford was most heavily besieged by traffic this was always a delightful backwater. The cobbled road surface was retained after a struggle in the 1960s, not least because it slowed down motorists.

3

North from St Giles'

Left: SS Philip & James' Church, the mother church of north Oxford, from Woodstock Road.
This fine Gothic church, designed by George Edmund Street and built between 1860 and 1862,
confirmed the highly respectable character of the developing Victorian suburb on the St John's College
estate. The coal merchant's cart outside the vicarage is a reminder that north Oxford houses were
prodigious consumers of coal, both for cooking and heating.
Right: Only the spire of the church is now visible above mature trees planted over a century ago.
The church of SS Philip & James was declared redundant as a parish church in 1982 and the listed
building now houses the Oxford Centre for Mission Studies. Woodstock Road is busy during the morning
and evening rush hours and bus lanes help to reduce journey times for Park-and-Ride buses.

Crowds at St Giles' Fair on a sunny afternoon, September 1907. The cabbies' shelter on the left has been commandeered as a temporary police station to ensure that the fair remains orderly and crime-free. First recorded as a parish wake in 1624, St Giles' Fair became a major attraction in the nineteenth century, catering not just for local people but also for hundreds of visitors brought to Oxford by special trains.

Today's fair-goers gather near the gallopers which always occupy pride of place near the Martyrs' Memorial. St Giles' Fair only lasts for two days in September but road markings and tall Victorian style street-lights are a reminder that St Giles is a busy thoroughfare on other days of the year. In the past there have been calls to move the fair, but these have always been successfully resisted.

Contrasts in St Giles, with steam-powered gallopers obscuring some of the street's fine eighteenth-century houses, 1895. The house on the left with the central pediment was built in 1702 for Thomas Rowney, MP for Oxford, and the Duke of Marlborough used it as his town house later in the eighteenth century. From 1852 it served as the judge's lodging when the Assize Courts were in session in Oxford.

The Superbowl ride and a Termineater van provide an even more improbable setting for the same immaculately preserved houses. The judge's lodging was last used for that purpose in 1965 and the building, now known as St Giles' House, has become part of St John's College.

Henry Hall's swing-boats at the northern end of St Giles' Fair, 1899. Steam power brought more noise to the fair and larger, more exciting rides, but there was still a place for these quieter entertainments. There is a glimpse of late seventeenth-century Black Hall through the trees on the right, and further north a tall Victorian block lords it over a much older three-gabled building.

The helter-skelter near Oxford's war memorial provides a more elevated view of the refreshment stalls and side-shows that now occupy this part of St Giles' Fair. The light brick and glass Mathematical Institute, designed by John Lankester, replaced the Victorian houses in 1964–6 and harmonises with gabled buildings dating originally from the early seventeenth century. Further on, university buildings of the 1960s in the Keble Road Triangle are of a very different character.

The western side of St Giles, looking north, 1907. Three-storey Georgian houses adorn a peaceful street scene peopled only by a few distant figures. The plane trees on the right were planted in 1859 following the removal of diseased elm trees the previous year.

Blackfriars and Pusey House replaced the Georgian houses south of Pusey Street, but further north St Giles is little changed. Blackfriars – nearest the camera – is a Dominican priory, which was designed by Doran Webb and built in the 1920s. Pusey House on the corner of Pusey Street was built as a theological centre in 1911–14. By 1925 car parking had formally taken over the tree-shaded margins of St Giles and motorists were at first charged 6*d* an hour for the privilege.

A woman with a parasol outside the St Giles' frontage of St John's College, 1880. Sir Thomas White had founded St John's in 1555 and the new college took over the fifteenth- and sixteenth-century buildings of the dissolved monastic foundation, St Bernard's College. This view shows the gabled Cook's Buildings of 1642–3 and an early seventeenth-century addition to the north.

With renewed or cleaned stonework, St John's College now presents a much crisper elevation to St Giles. Parked cars occupy much of the foreground but trees still flourish in the walled enclosure in front of the college.

The Front Quad at St John's College, 1870. St John's inherited the quad from St Bernard's College and the north range contains the hall and college chapel. Battlements were added to the buildings in 1617 and in the eighteenth century sash windows replaced older windows around much of the quad.

The replacement of decayed Headington stone has restored the architectural details of the Front Quad and a few chimneys have vanished, marking the general passing of coal fires for heating. A clock was added as a war memorial above the passage between hall and chapel in 1919. Luxuriant growth masks the hall window and the gravel quad is now paved and laid to lawn.

The temporary chapel and hall of Keble College, early 1870s. The college was founded as a memorial to John Keble (d. 1866), a central figure in the Oxford Movement. It was the first of its large-scale polychrome brick buildings, designed by William Butterfield, and was erected between 1868 and 1870. This unadorned brick structure was situated on the south side of what became Liddon Quad.

Undergraduates play croquet in Liddon Quad in the shadow of Keble's massive dining hall and library, which were designed by Butterfield and completed in 1878. Keble College chapel, also by Butterfield, was built in the north-east corner of Liddon Quad between 1873 and 1876.

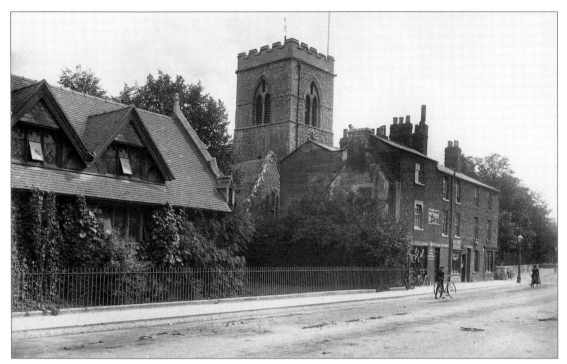

St Giles' Church from Woodstock Road, 1906. The early thirteenth-century church tower rises above houses and the gabled parish room. The latter was quite a recent building, designed by local architect Harry Wilkinson Moore and built in 1887–91, but luxuriant planting already masked it by the time of this photograph.

The buildings are little changed, and although the parish room is slightly more visible, not least because of the wartime removal of railings for salvage, the tower of St Giles' Church is almost lost in the trees.

The Woodstock Road frontage of the Radcliffe Infirmary in 1890. John Radcliffe (1652–1714) had been physician to William III and Queen Anne and the trust fund that he endowed helped to build this county hospital between 1759 and 1770. The Georgian building, originally with a first-floor entrance, was designed by Stiff Leadbetter; Arthur Blomfield added the Gothic-style chapel in 1864.

The main building of the Radcliffe Infirmary is closer to its original appearance after re-facing of the stonework, but with the main entrance now on the ground floor, a large window occupies the site of the first-floor doorway. The Georgian-style three-storey range on the left was added in 1913, serving as the outpatients' department until most of the infirmary's services were transferred to the new John Radcliffe Hospital in 1979.

A glimpse of North Oxford before development, *c.* 1858. The view is from Woodstock Road along Jeffrey's Lane, the site of Bevington Road, towards distant Banbury Road. Stephen Jeffrey's Globe Nursery was just to the north and the woman in the foreground may be his daughter, Miriam Jeffrey, who became Taunt's wife in 1863. The bosky landscape behind her was unpopulated, but intrepid middle-class folk had in fact been building and occupying villas nearby for several decades.

The backs of Victorian Gothic semi-detached villas in Bevington Road are now glimpsed between 80 Woodstock Road and new buildings for St Anne's College. St John's College had Bevington Road laid out as part of the development of its north Oxford estate in the 1860s. Earlier gravel digging had left the site considerably lower than the Banbury or Woodstock roads and that feature is still evident today.

A view from the tennis court in Lady Margaret Hall, late 1890s. This women's hall was founded in 1878 and Old Hall, the plain brick building in the distance, was its first home – and a draughty one, by all accounts. Basil Champneys added a Queen Anne-style extension in 1881–3 and Wordsworth, nearest the camera, was a grander addition, designed by Sir Reginald Blomfield and built in 1896.

Wordsworth has a new eaves cornice and lost its roof-top balustrade, and informal gardens have ousted the tennis players. A long range called Lodge filled the gap between Wordsworth and Basil Champneys' building in 1926, echoing the William-and-Mary style chosen by Blomfield thirty years earlier.

Farndon Road, looking towards Woodstock Road, 1900s. This sinuous road, laid out in the 1870s, formed a link between the artisan houses of Kingston Road and the grand villas in Woodstock Road. Restrictive covenants in college building leases helped to maintain the atmosphere of peace and quiet and to keep anything that smacked of trade out of the best areas.

Well-planted front gardens are now more popular than creeper-clad houses, and the broad carriageway, formerly disturbed only by the occasional tradesman's vehicle, is now lined by residents' cars. Electric street-lighting has ousted the gaslamps but a hexagonal Victorian pillar-box survives on the corner of Warnborough Road.

St Barnabas' Church from the Walton Well Road railway bridge, 1914. The London and North Western Railway Company's line from Bletchley to Oxford was completed in 1851, crossing the former navigation stream of the River Thames by a very low bridge in the foreground. St Barnabas' Church, designed by Arthur Blomfield, was built to serve the working-class suburb of Jericho in 1868–72.

Trees now hide St Barnabas' Church from Walton Well Road: this part of the old London and North Western line was abandoned in the 1950s when Oxford's rail services were concentrated at the former Great Western station. The disused line nearly became the site of a major relief road in the 1960s, and more recently there have been plans for a guided bus expressway along the route.

Looking east along Polstead Road, *c.* 1910. Polstead Road was formed in 1887 as the St John's College estate extended steadily northwards. Large semi-detached houses were built behind the low brick walls and iron railings that were prescribed throughout the estate. Lime trees were planted on the pavement edge in the 1890s as a result of a beautification campaign by the local curate, the Revd Robert Hartley.

Regular pruning has preserved Mr Hartley's lime trees into the twenty-first century, but the street's iron railings went for salvage in the Second World War. No. 2 Polstead Road was the boyhood home of T.E. Lawrence (1888–1935), who became famous as Lawrence of Arabia during the First World War.

Godstow Road in Lower Wolvercote, looking east towards the Green, 1910. Wolvercote was still a country village outside the city boundary but its paper mill, substantially rebuilt in the 1890s, introduced an industrial element and the Victorian houses in the foreground have an urban feel. Wolvercote had its own railway halt from 1908, further encouraging the building of new houses in the village.

Wolvercote became a part of Oxford City in 1929 and one early consequence was a greater expenditure on roads, pavements and street-lighting. Some old properties were demolished as slums and the thatched cottages visible in 1910 were replaced by the row of houses set back from Godstow Road.

The Grapes Inn at Yarnton, 1916. The Grapes dates back to the eighteenth century and formerly stood beside a toll-gate called Peyman's Gate on the turnpike road between Oxford and Woodstock. Verdant Green, the hero of a mid-nineteenth-century Oxford novel by Cuthbert Bede, and his three friends, are intercepted here by the University Proctor while returning the worse for wear from the Bear Hotel in Woodstock.

The Grapes is now the Turnpike with a punning inn sign illustrating a turning pike. Externally, the building is little changed, but traffic on the main road is heavy at peak times and there is a roundabout nearby at the junction with the Yarnton Road. An unobtrusive car park north of the inn caters for today's visitors to the Turnpike.

Yarnton village and post office, 1917. The post office on the left occupied part of the clerk's house and schoolroom, built in 1817 by Alderman William Fletcher of Oxford. The local wheelwright lived in the three-storey house on the right with his workshop next door. Beyond the junction of Cassington Road and Rutten Lane, the Stocks Trees were large elm trees on a little green near the site of the parish stocks.

The Stocks Trees have gone and road improvements have swept away much of the green, revealing more of Jackson's farmhouse beyond Rutten Lane. The well-restored clerk's house and schoolroom has lost its chimney stacks and the former wheelwright's house and workshop are now modern family homes.

Cassington village and green, 1916. A tranquil scene of thatched stone houses and tall elm trees in a village set in the flat Thames Valley landscape just 6 miles from Oxford. The building on the right was the smithy.

Cassington today with older houses modernised and their roofs tiled rather than thatched; new properties in sympathetic style have filled gaps between the buildings. The smithy has vanished and lime trees have replaced the elms on the green. The road through the village has been widened and more clearly defined to cope with increased traffic.

Sidney Smith's premises in Lyne Road, Kidlington, 1905. Smith flourished here as a carpenter, wheelwright and undertaker from the mid-1890s, typically combining a range of crafts that all required woodworking skills. Men are hard at work outside the workshop and a donkey cart is ready to carry away some of the firm's products.

Smith passed the business on to his son Ben, and S.W. Smith & Sons were still trading as timber merchants in the village on the eve of the Second World War. Lyne House is now a private house and it has been enlarged with extra dormer windows and a two-storey extension on the site of the workshop.

A lively scene on the Banbury Road in Kidlington, 1904. Two men are engaged in deep discussion while a woman pushes a pram and various children keep their eyes firmly fixed on the photographer. The Black Bull on the right was built in about 1870 to replace an earlier building at the end of High Street. The Black Horse pub sign is visible further up the road.

Banbury Road is now a busy main road and this junction, though quieter since the opening of the M40, is no place for the pedestrian to loiter. The Black Bull still flourishes, as does the Black Horse. The western end of High Street has been pedestrianised and the wooden hanging-basket holders, dubbed crucifixes by local critics, were part of an environmental improvement scheme. A good-looking housing development of the 1980s occupies the corner of Banbury Road and Lyne Road.

High Street, Kidlington, 1904. The local postman, Jim Gardner, is thought to be the man posed in the foreground. This part of High Street was known as 'The Hill' and the fence on the left leads the eye down towards the distant spire of St Mary's Church. Behind the postman, Bateman's shop can be seen on the corner of the Moors.

The church spire is still just visible from High Street but it has more competition from trees, telegraph poles and lampposts. The gate and overhanging trees on the far side of the road are all part of 95 High Street, a three-storey stone house dating from the mid-nineteenth century. A functional but inelegant pavement provides pedestrian access to houses built since the 1930s on the south side of the road.

St Mary's Church, Kidlington, and village houses, 1904. The slender fourteenth-century spire is a notable feature of the church, visible from afar across the flat Cherwell Valley landscape. Attractive stone houses dating from the seventeenth and eighteenth centuries complement the view, recalling an earlier time when Kidlington was an apricot village, sending large quantities to Covent Garden market in London.

A war memorial stands on the edge of the churchyard and, after another century of growth, the yew trees mask more of St Mary's Church. The Church Street houses are little changed externally with just the odd chimney-stack removed, but there is perhaps more planting in the gardens and less on the house walls.

4

East from St Clement's

Left: Members of the Morrell family celebrating the christening of Herbert William James,
the son of James Herbert and Julia Morrell at Headington Hill Hall, September 1915.
An earlier James Morrell, the Oxford brewer, had acquired the estate in the 1850s, and John Thomas
designed the substantial new Hall (1857–8), which is partially visible in the background.
Right: Oxford Brookes University employees strike a more informal pose on the same flight of steps.
Headington Hill Hall remained the home of the Morrell family until 1939. Oxford City Council
acquired the property in 1953, and in 1959 leased the house and grounds to Robert Maxwell for
99 years; as Maxwell became an increasingly controversial figure, the hall was sometimes
described as the finest council house in England! Oxford Brookes University acquired the lease
of the house in 1993.

High Street, St Clement's, east of York Place during the annual St Clement's Fair, when people and stalls filled the street outside Richard Hatton's boot and clothing store, September 1910. St Clement's Fair was first recorded in the eighteenth century as a toy fair and, unlike the better-known St Giles' Fair held earlier in the month, it remained very much a small-scale local event.

St Clement's Street today is a busy road and the foreground is dominated by Anchor Court on the left and modern brick-built houses on the right. Two gabled buildings further along preserve part of the old street frontage and, beyond the bend in the road, many nineteenth-century properties survive. Now, as then, a tree overhangs the road from the forecourt of the Black Horse.

Marston Lane, looking north towards New Marston, 17 August 1892. The city boundary had been extended in 1889 and a large crowd has assembled to see off the mayoral party, visible beyond the hedge, which was beating the new bounds for the first time. The beaters were heading up the path behind Headington Hill Hall towards Pullen's Lane.

The view still appears rural but Marston Road was widened in the late 1930s, taking away much of the generous footway. The hedge on the far side of the road masked temporary government buildings which occupied open fields during the Second World War and have only recently been cleared for an Oxford Brookes University development. A spectacular Islamic Centre for Oxford University is being completed behind the fence on the left.

Beaters of the bounds crossing Pullen's Lane, 17 August 1892. They were passing Joe Pullen's Tree, an elm that was said to have been planted in about 1680 by the Revd Josiah Pullen (1631–1714), Vice-President of Magdalen Hall, who enjoyed a daily walk up Headington Hill, savouring the view of Oxford from this point. According to one story, the tree sprouted from a walking stick that he had stuck in the ground.

The decayed remains of Joe Pullen's tree were finally destroyed by fire on 13 October 1909, and a tablet on the brick wall beside the dog walker commemorates the tree. Despite the growth of Oxford, Pullen's Lane retains a rural character and is still a private road.

The south front of the Manor House at Headington, 1913. One of a number of grand eighteenth-century houses in the village, the Manor House was built in 1779 for Sir Banks Jenkinson, 6th Baronet of Walcot. The building accommodated a school for young ladies in the mid-nineteenth century but it had become a private house again, the home of Colonel Hoole, when this photograph was taken.

The Radcliffe Infirmary purchased the extensive Manor House estate in 1919 in order to build a tuberculosis hospital on this healthy hilltop site. This proved a far-sighted and fateful decision, leading since the 1970s to the gradual concentration of most local hospital facilities at the new John Radcliffe Hospital. The Manor House now provides office accommodation in a quiet corner of this busy complex.

Thatched stone cottages dating from the seventeenth century in Church Street, Old Headington, 1915. Headington had a dubious reputation in the seventeenth and eighteenth centuries, but a resident vicar from the 1860s and a growing number of wealthy landowners helped to generate a new respectability, which is evident in this tranquil photograph.

A new terrace set back from the road replaced the thatched cottages in 1938, and St Andrew's Road today is a peaceful and attractive part of the Old Headington Conservation Area. Retained lamp-standards with Winsor lanterns and the careful redevelopment of Laurel Farm on the right in the 1980s have helped to maintain a village character which is compromised only by traffic signs and yellow lines.

High Street, Old Headington, looking north towards Church Street, 1915. Eighteenth-century cottages built of stone from local quarries lead the eye down towards tall lime, or linden, trees outside Linden House. The garden of the Bell pub lay behind the wall on the left.

The row of cottages on the right has been lost, probably because of their pinched dimensions, but most old properties in Old High Street have survived and the lime trees still remain. The Bell pub closed in about 1992 and the older rear part of the building is now a private house. The changes seem minor in the context of large-scale development that led to Headington becoming part of Oxford in 1929. Nearby London Road, by contrast, is a busy main road and shopping centre.

Headington Quarry Morris Men outside the Chequers in Headington Quarry, 1899. Percy Manning, a lecturer at the university and researcher into local folklore, had organised the revival of the Morris at Quarry in 1898. The newly revived side danced here on 26 June 1899 and Taunt, another enthusiast for old customs, was there to record the proceedings.

The Chequers' temporary landlord stands outside the pub where the Headington Quarry Morris Men are still regularly seen and heard. William Kimber, the fiddler of the Morris side photographed by Taunt, lived on in Headington until his death at the age of 89 in 1961.

A man with a pony and trap at the top of Shotover Hill, 1913. This was part of the main road between Oxford and London until the 1770s and coach passengers leaving the University City had to get out and walk up the steep hill; in December 1690 the death of Dr Matthew Slade, aged 63, in a coach bound for Wheatley was attributed to the effects of 'his violent motion going up Shotover Hill on foot'.

Shotover is now a country park providing some 400 acres of readily accessible countryside on the high ground to the east of Oxford. The footpath off to the right leads down the hill towards Headington Quarry.

Looking north along Forest Hill village street, 1907. The activities of the photographer have attracted the attention of a number of local people who are watching curiously from the roadway, the raised footway and their cottage gardens. The houses, some of them with thatched roofs, would have been built of stone from local quarries.

The thatched house on the right, considerably modernised and improved, is among the older properties to have survived in a much leafier Forest Hill. The village street has had to be widened at this point, claiming old rubble stone walls, and there are access roads to modern houses on both sides.

Wheatley stone quarries, 1887, showing the distant spire of St Mary's Church, which had been completed in 1868. Earlier in the century Wheatley had been a rowdy place and the conical lock-up, just visible at the right of the picture, must have had many occupants; it was built by Cooper, a local mason, in 1834.

Templars Close was built in this part of the old quarry in the 1960s and the area by the lock-up is now a children's recreation ground.

Looking west along High Street, Wheatley, 1887. Two-storey stone and tiled houses with brick chimneys line a street that was part of the main London–Oxford road until 1775. The house on the right has external hinged shutters, needed perhaps as an extra defence against noisy or otherwise unpleasant activities at the premises opposite.

Shrubs and trees overhang the boundary walls of properties in today's more prosperous Wheatley. Brick-built houses on the right have replaced the stone house with the shutters but Chillingworth House on the left and Oxford House on the right survived long enough to be updated and cherished. Electric street-lighting is a modern benefit but High Street tends to be a traffic rat-run on weekdays.

Looking up Church Road towards the village school in Horspath, 1914. The school was founded in 1856 and had been much extended with a large classroom and a teacher's house beside the road. There is a glimpse of the Manor House, which was largely rebuilt in Victorian times, on the right beside the footway.

Housing development has partially obscured the school, which still occupies its old premises. New classrooms have been added and the school has attractive grounds behind the hedge on the left. The view on the right is little changed and there is still a touch of rural informality about the footway outside.

Horspath village green and distant Shotover Hill, from the railway embankment beside Horspath halt, 1908. A goat grazes peacefully beyond a series of wooden poles that would have turned the area into a drying ground and meeting place on washdays.

Horspath lost its halt when the line between Oxford and Princes Risborough was closed in 1963. With the original site now inaccessible, this view is from the surviving railway bridge further east. A mower rather than a goat keeps the grass cut these days and a brick and tiled bus shelter covered with creeper now serves as a potential meeting place.

Two little girls pass the time of day on the green in Garsington, August 1902. Open windows and distant washing on the line suggest a hot summer's day; the Three Horseshoes, set back from the road but picked out by its pub sign, was probably doing a good trade.

Rectory Cottage on the right and some of the other old properties on the green have been modernised and extended as cars have increased the appeal of country living. The Three Horseshoes is still in business behind the tree on the right. Concrete kerbs, driveways and carefully tended verges give the street a tidier image.

Garsington children gather round and clamber on the medieval village cross, probably during local celebrations of the coronation of Edward VII, August 1902. The view behind them extends down to Rectory Cottage.

No children or adults are in evidence today as the cross is revealed to consist of an octagonal base on three stone steps with a modern shaft. The growth of rural traffic has changed the character of the road, requiring a definite separation between vehicles and pedestrians where formerly none was needed.

Spectators watch a demonstration at the Oxford Military College in Cowley during a visit by the Duke of Cambridge, 1890. The college was established in 1876 to train boys for commissions in the Army and the incomplete South Range seen here was part of T.G. Jackson's ambitious scheme for a huge quadrangle. The small building on the right was a laboratory added in 1882.

A successful development by Berkeley Homes in 1999 restored the surviving Military College buildings and filled the gaps with tall gabled blocks of appropriate design. The college closed in 1896 after a long struggle and the buildings were later converted to industrial use. William Morris manufactured his first Bullnose Morris cars here from 1913 and adapted the buildings in the 1920s for the Morris Oxford, later the Nuffield, Press. The Nuffield Press operated on the site until 1995.

Looking down from Lye Hill towards Marsh Lane, 1914. The track leads down to Barracks Lane, marked by a fence and a hedgerow, with the wide open spaces of Cowley Marsh beyond. College sporting clubs used the marsh extensively for cricket and football and the University Golf Club practised there from the 1870s until the 1920s.

The growth of scrub on Lye Hill has made necessary this lower viewpoint south of Barracks Lane. Marsh Road is partially hidden by the large City Council depot, which occupied the site of a wartime hutted camp in the 1960s. A goalpost indicates the continuing recreational use of the marsh but housing development along Cowley Road – demonstrated by the three-storey building on the right – has substantially encroached on what was once a large open space.

Bartlemas Road from the tower of SS Mary and John Church in Cowley Road, 1907. The Bartlemas estate was laid out for building in 1891 by the Oxford & Provident Land & Building Society, and houses soon occupied the attractive well-drained site. Prominent adverts for Oxo, Quaker Oats and other products cover the blank side wall of 237 Cowley Road, then occupied by Richard Pether, cricket-bat maker.

Axtell's stone masonry yard occupied the corner site next to No. 237 for many years, but Focus 4 Health, an alternative medicine centre, now occupies modern premises there. Along Bartlemas Road, Velux roof lights and dormer windows indicate the conversion of lofts into living space. Parked cars occupy much of the road during the day and, as back gardens have matured, trees have become a more prominent feature.

Oxford workhouse from Cowley Road, 1916. The large brick building was erected in 1863–5 to replace an earlier workhouse on the site of Wellington Square. As the sentry on the gate suggests, the workhouse had been taken over by the military during the First World War, becoming part of the Third Southern General Hospital, which looked after casualties from the Front.

Oxford's workhouse evolved into Cowley Road Hospital in 1948 and became a respected geriatric hospital before its closure in 1980. The site was cleared for a housing development in 1986, leaving only the workhouse chapel, which has become an Asian cultural centre. The access road is now called Manzil Way, meaning 'destiny' in Hindi and Urdu, and a mosque, the minaret of which is visible above the trees, is nearing completion. The land in the foreground has been laid out as a small park.

5

South from New Hinksey

Left: Flooding on the Great Western Railway line north of Red Bridge on the Abingdon Road in November 1894. Rail services between Oxford and Didcot were cut off for several days and these railway employees were using an inspection trolley to assess damage to the trackbed. Outlying houses in New Hinksey are visible in the distance.

Right: A London-bound passenger train approaches Red Bridge through Oxford's less intensively managed urban fringe. Railway lines to the left were laid in 1943 when a huge area of sidings called Oxford South yard was built in the run up to D-Day to help marshal trainloads of military traffic bound for the south coast. Part of the yard is now a Network Rail depot.

Lake Street, probably during the floods of November 1894. The little suburb of New Hinksey dated back to 1847 and this street took its name from the nearby Railway Lake, a large pit caused by gravel excavations during the building of the Great Western railway line through Oxford. Like other low-lying areas of the city, New Hinksey flooded quite regularly at this time.

Lake Street's terraced houses have been successfully adapted for modern living and parked cars have taken over the road and even the pavement. The former general shop on the corner of Gordon Street and the Crown at 23 Lake Street have both become private houses. Improved river management has greatly reduced the incidence of flooding in New Hinksey.

Workmen washing sand for the filter beds at the city waterworks off Abingdon Road, 1914. The waterworks opened here in 1856, initially pumping unfiltered water into people's homes from the Railway Lake. Turning on the tap could be a biology lesson – Taunt was among the critics who fought for filtration, which was introduced in 1883.

With the completion of a new city waterworks at Swinford in 1934, the old site became redundant. The filter beds were converted into swimming pools of varying depths for Hinksey Baths, a lido that opened in 1936. In recent years the nearest one has been adapted for ball games as people's appetite for swimming in cool water has diminished. Former waterworks buildings survive in the background and mature trees planted in that era flourish around the site.

A wooden footbridge on the pathway from New Hinksey to South Hinksey, 1909. The raised causeway across the Thames floodplain is popularly known as the Devil's Backbone, presumably because local people thought that no human agency could have constructed this spine-like feature.

A more robust iron footbridge now carries the causeway over the Hinksey Stream of the River Thames. This low-lying area has remained undeveloped and is a crucial part of Oxford's green setting. The overgrown hedge in the background forms the boundary of the wartime Oxford South railway yard.

Manor Road, South Hinksey, 1909. These tall limestone-rubble buildings dating perhaps from the late seventeenth or early eighteenth century were agricultural cottages belonging to the Earl of Abingdon at this time.

Manor Road is no longer a mudbath in winter and 1 Myrtle Cottage, on the left, has been extended to provide extra living space. The village location still appears peaceful but the busy A34 is just behind the camera, generating traffic noise day and night.

Chilswell Farm above South Hinksey, 1895. The stone farmhouse is masked by other farm buildings including the thatched single-storey range on the right. The horse-drawn open carriage and the men nearby seem to be waiting for something to happen.

Chilswell Farm, tucked away down a lane off Foxcombe Road, is no longer a working farm. Old buildings are currently being converted and new ones added to turn the complex into a desirable housing scheme.

Old houses in Kennington Road, Kennington, *c.* 1900. Jasmine Cottage on the right is a thatched rubble stone building dating back to the seventeenth century. Further up the road, opposite the entrance to Cow Lane, an attractive property of similar age has a jettied timber-framed wing.

Jasmine Cottage still overlooks Kennington Road but the other property has regrettably been demolished. The road has been widened as the community has grown and traffic levels have increased, but rough grass verges and rubble stone walls preserve the village character. The Walled Garden, a new development just round the corner on the left, includes new thatched houses.

Back view of Minchery Farm, Littlemore, 1904. This stone building, incorporating early sixteenth-century work, was originally part of a Benedictine priory, founded here in about 1150. The religious house was dissolved like so many others in the reign of Henry VIII but this building was retained as a farmhouse only to become part of the city's sewage farm in the 1870s.

Minchery Farm housed sewage-farm employees and then became a nightclub for a time in the 1970s. Today it is the Priory pub at the heart of the huge Ozone Leisure Park, begun in 2000, which includes Oxford United's Kassam Stadium, a nine-screen multiplex cinema, a bingo hall and bowling alley and a hotel.

An animated scene in Sandford Road, Littlemore, 1900s. People have gathered on both sides of the road outside the George pub and by the junction with Railway Lane. Tall trees on the right mark the entrance to Lawn Upton House and, in the distance, the Marlborough Head is visible on the corner of the Oxford and Cowley roads.

Both road and pavement are now made up and the raised road surface outside the houses has been pared down. Garages have replaced the first pair of houses but the Old House survives and the George still flourishes. Sandford Road was a busy main road until the completion of the Oxford ring road in 1966 and, in the distance, a new Marlborough Head pub, now Blewitt Court, was built in 1940 to capture a larger slice of that passing trade.

Thatched cottages in Railway Lane, Littlemore, 1903. Like many village streets at this time, the lane was totally unmade-up, a quagmire for much of the winter and a dustbowl in summer. Beyond the cottages on the right, a gable end with three narrow ventilation slits is part of a stone barn of *c*. 1700. The village post office is visible on the left beyond Chapel Lane.

The road surface looks little better today and the view is dominated by a wooden fence protecting a development site on the left. Some old properties have gone but others survive, including the stone barn and the old post office in the distance. The fine rubble stone wall on the right, now topped with a fence, helps to secure the premises of the Littlemore Scientific Engineering Company.

Children carrying May garlands through Iffley, 1906. The ancient custom was often an excuse for begging and general misbehaviour but this was a modern, sanitised version in which well-dressed schoolchildren collected for charity. They were pupils at Iffley village school, the thatched stone building in the background that had been erected in 1838. Court House on the left, dating perhaps from the seventeenth century, was probably the original farmhouse of Court Farm.

Despite Iffley's becoming part of Oxford City in 1929, Church Way at the heart of the Iffley conservation area still looks like a village street. The old school closed in 1961 but the building, with retained bell turret and restored thatch, is now a community hall. Court House is little altered externally and the view is much enhanced by retained rubble stone walls and old stone kerbs.

Henley House and adjoining villas in Iffley Road, 1905. This large Victorian Gothic house, built for H.E. Abrams, was built on the corner of Henley Street in 1887. Abrams opted for the projecting porch to avoid the 'damp corners' that resulted from putting porches and bay windows too close together. Iffley Road was the most fashionable part of Victorian east Oxford and tall villas like this offered fine views across the Thames Valley towards Hinksey Hill.

The same properties today, shaved of the creepers that were a Victorian and Edwardian fashion, to reveal details such as Gothic arched windows and ornamental bargeboards in the gables. Since 1977 this area of Iffley Road has been part of a conservation area designed to protect its unique character.

6

West from Park End Street

Left: The road through North Hinksey, 1885. The area round this picturesque stone and thatched cottage was lovingly described by John Ruskin, Slade Professor of Fine Art, when he set his undergraduates to improve the village road in 1874 and experience for themselves 'the pleasure of useful muscular work'.

Right: Ruskin Cottage, complete now with a thatched porch, still graces North Hinksey village, and a plaque on the front of the house records the road-making episode. Ruskin would probably not like the look of the tarmac road, practical as it may be, but the roadside verge is still happily unkempt and the village has avoided yellow lines.

Park End Street, looking west from Pacey's Bridge, 1920. Park End Street is a continuation of New Road and the two formed part of a completely new western exit from the city built in 1770. The street was named after a colliery in the Forest of Dean which supplied coal to a nearby wharf in the early nineteenth century. Sandwiched between the canal and the railway, it was at the heart of industrial and commercial Oxford.

After enduring decades of heavy traffic, Park End Street has become a quieter place since the changes introduced by the Oxford Transport Strategy in 1999. Once well known for garages such as Hartwells, Coxeter's, King's and Layton's and for Ward's department store, the street is now geared to leisure needs with bars, restaurants and a club. Scaffolding on the left marks the redevelopment of the old Coxeter's site as apartments and student accommodation.

Frank Cooper's Victoria Buildings in Park End Street, 1906. Frank Cooper was in business as an Italian warehouseman in High Street. His famous Oxford marmalade was launched accidentally in 1874 when his wife Sarah made too much for the family and the surplus flew off the shelves. These premises were opened in 1903 in order to increase production and the photograph shows yet another consignment of marmalade leaving the factory.

Victoria Buildings today from Frideswide Square, the pedestrian area created during controversial alterations to the road layout near Oxford station in 1998–9. Frank Cooper Ltd added a two-storey wing to their factory in 1929 but moved all production to the old ice rink in Botley Road in 1950. The Victoria Buildings became county council offices for many years and later housed an antiques centre called the Old Jam Factory; offices and a bar now occupy the premises.

Oxford's railway stations during the floods of November 1875. The Great Western Railway station opened in 1852 and its overall roof is visible in the background with part of the train shed of the London & North Western Railway station away to the right. The foreground is occupied by a group of stranded passengers and two of the enterprising punt-owners who ran an impromptu water-taxi service.

A daily tide of motor vehicles now ebbs and flows through this junction and a complex series of traffic lights monitors both this main route and the bus lane away to the left. The original Great Western Railway station lost its overall roof during alterations in 1890–1 and the rest of the building was demolished in 1969–70. The present utilitarian building, with a bus interchange and extensive cycle parking, dates from 1990.

Osney Abbey and Mill, 1911. The stone building with a high pitched roof had been built in the late fifteenth century as part of a long riverside range and it represents the last above-ground remnant of Osney Abbey, a great Augustinian house founded in 1127. The abbey was dissolved in 1538 but its mill, dating back to the twelfth century, survived, and, as the brick chimney suggests, it had become a modern flour mill by the time of this photograph.

A glimpse of the surviving abbey building from the bridge across the Osney millstream. Osney Mill was destroyed by fire in 1946, and while the future use of historic buildings on the site has remained uncertain for years, the former millstream has become the focal point of a marina.

The Black Horse pub at Botley, 1921. Botley developed around a watermill on the Seacourt Stream, a branch of the Thames, and as a roadside settlement beside roads from Oxford to the west that became much more important in the eighteenth and nineteenth centuries. New houses appeared and the Black Horse, built in *c.* 1840, catered for both local and passing trade. The pub became the Botley terminus for the No. 6 bus from Cowley in 1914.

West Way at an unusually quiet moment showing bus shelters on both sides of the road. Berkshire County Council widened this section of the main road into Oxford as part of a joint venture with Oxford City in 1923–4 but since the 1960s traffic congestion here has become almost a daily feature. Commercial development has claimed older properties including the Black Horse, which closed in 1963 and was pulled down in 1991.

Old Botley, looking north from North Hinksey Lane towards distant Seacourt Farm, 1921. Until local turnpike-road improvements bypassed the village in the 1760s, the main road between Oxford and Botley emerged between the house on the right and the row of cottages beyond it. The wooden building beside the cottages was a laundry by this time, having previously been a blacksmith's workshop and then a mission room.

Surviving properties on the right provide a point of reference in a much altered scene. Seacourt Farm was demolished in the 1960s for the building of Seacourt Tower – sometimes described as Botley Cathedral. Modern offices adjoining the tower have replaced Hartford Motors' car showroom. The site of demolished properties beyond the cottages provided an enlarged car park for the Carpenters Arms pub, which is now a McDonald's restaurant.

There are distant glimpses of two surviving thatched houses but detached 1960s houses replaced old stone cottages on the right. A dead straight road now crosses the green, and property entrances have levelled the raised bank which provided spectators with a grandstand view of the labouring undergraduates.

Ruskin's road-menders, watched by a small audience, work on the green at North Hinksey, 1874. The undergraduates were supervised by Ruskin's gardener and their activities attracted national media attention and a degree of ridicule. They may not have created the perfect road but a surveyor working for the local landowner, Colonel Harcourt, reported that 'the gentlemen had done little harm'.

Dean Court with a woman driving her pony and trap towards Eynsham, 1885. The outbuildings of Dean Court Farm are visible behind the tree on the left. In 1814 this route was improved to become the turnpike road between Eynsham and Oxford replacing the older route through Wytham Woods, which had been a haunt of highwaymen.

Trees, shrubs and hedges combine to mask the scale of modern housing development along Eynsham Road while cycle lane and centre line markings hint at busier moments in peak hours. The Cumnor Hill bypass, part of the A420, now crosses the Eynsham Road just round the corner.

The junction of High Street and Leys Road in Cumnor, 1912. The Unitarian church, partly obscured by a massive tree, was built in 1895 as a result of subscriptions by members of the George Street Congregational Church in Oxford. Leys Road continues past the early nineteenth-century row of cottages towards the Physic Well and Bablockhythe.

The loss of the tree and an altered road layout have substantially changed the look of this corner. The overspill parking space in the foreground is linked to the village hall opposite, which is just out of the picture. The brick-built church is now Cumnor United Reformed Church and neighbouring terraced houses in Leys Road have been successfully adapted by the addition of dormer windows and roof-lights.

Cumnor village pond in Appleton Road, 1912. There are thatched houses dating back to the seventeenth century beyond the pond and a track to the left curves away towards Rockley Farm House. The house opposite with its gable end to the street was the village post office in the 1870s.

The pond today is more of a visual amenity than a feature of everyday significance in village life. Older properties have been modernised and new houses with tiled roofs and dormer windows have been built in Appleton Road beyond the pond. Distant elms have perished and clipped hedges give the village a more orderly appearance.

Curious spectators watch men erecting telegraph poles in High Street, Cumnor, 1912. Part of Manor Farm is visible on the right and, on the left, beyond the thatched stone cottage, there are glimpses of the village school. The turning for both the village pond and Appleton is at the far end of the street.

The view has scarcely changed although a one way system is now needed to direct traffic around the heart of the village. It is tempting to speculate that the creeper-clad pole beyond Manor Farm is the one that was being put up in 1912. The old school buildings now accommodate a post office and village stores as well as a community hall. Decorative thatched pheasants adorn the roof of the cottage on the left.

A social outing at the Greyhound pub in Besselsleigh, 1908. The revellers were members of the Ancient Order of Foresters, a friendly society established for mutual aid in times of hardship, sickness or bereavement. The Greyhound, dating from the eighteenth century, was an attractive first stop for travellers heading out of Oxford on the main road to Faringdon.

The Greyhound is now a popular pub restaurant mercifully set back a little from the busy A420. The horse-chestnut tree still frames the stone building, which has exchanged the creeper of a century ago for window boxes, hanging baskets and wall-mounted lanterns.

7

By River & Canal

Left: King's Weir above Godstow, 1870. This weir was first mentioned in 1541, and despite talk in 1817 about installing a pound lock, the weir with a single pair of gates remained throughout the nineteenth century. The weir-keeper worked from a little cabin and the cottage and garden on the far bank were privately occupied.
Right: The Thames Conservancy built a pound lock at King's Weir in 1928 and provided the neat stone lock house for a resident lock-keeper at the same time. The location is still quite remote but within earshot of the busy A34, built as Oxford's western bypass in 1960.

A team of horses prepares to haul timber away from a field beside the Thames towpath at Godstow, 1880. The Trout Inn is visible in the background behind spindly elm trees and the stone bridge of 1780 that carried the Wytham Road across a new navigation cut.

A modern bridge now crosses the widened navigation stream and the Trout is completely hidden by trees. A chain and post barrier prevents boats from going down the side channel, which leads to a weir beside the inn.

The Trout Inn at Godstow, *c.* 1880. There was probably an inn here by 1625, but today's building is largely the result of rebuilding in 1737. The inn is first recorded by name as the Trout in 1861, and in Victorian times it was a favourite destination for respectable boating parties from Oxford.

The Trout remains hugely popular, catering for a greater number of customers on the widened riverside terrace and in a single storey extension. Many people come by car but the inn is also handy for walkers and for boat users from the main river.

Bossoms Boatyard still flourishes at Medley and manages this marina on the side channel between the towpath and Port Meadow. Rowing boats are no longer hired out here but the nearby Medley Sailing Club, founded in 1937, ensures that sailing dinghies are a regular sight.

Rival boatyards at Medley in 1880. The Bossoms and Beesleys were two old Oxford families who had worked on and around the river for centuries and now competed for business on this attractive site beside Port Meadow. Many people, including Lewis Carroll on his famous voyage with Alice in 1862, preferred outings on the upper river because it was quieter than the Thames below Folly Bridge.

Medley Weir, *c.* 1880. Like many other weirs on the upper Thames, Medley was still a flash weir and the weir-keeper had to dismantle part of the structure and swing back the bridge to allow boats to pass through. A boat travelling downstream had then to be steered safely through the gap but going upstream required hard haulage work by men or horses.

The Thames Conservancy built the single-storey house on the left for the weir-keeper in 1904 but subsequently removed the weir in 1928. Beyond and to the right of the towpath bridge there is a glimpse of the Bailey bridge across a side channel of the Thames to Port Meadow. Royal Engineers constructed this bridge in 1946 to replace the Victorian Sheriff's bridge, which had been washed away by floods.

A view of St Barnabas' Church from the west, 1920. The suburb of Jericho, probably so called because of its relative remoteness, originated in the 1820s and its residents included printing workers, railway families and college servants. William Ward, a local coal merchant, gave the site for St Barnabas' Church and Thomas Combe, Superintendent of the University Press, paid for the building, which was designed by Arthur Blomfield and built in 1868–72.

St Barnabas' Church from the Oxford canal towpath, showing narrowboats and the backs of Victorian houses in St Barnabas' Street. The church tower was re-roofed with a lower pitch in 1893. The boatyard, now to be replaced by a housing development, occupied former coal wharves that had literally fuelled the city until the Clean Air Act of 1956 led to the creation of smokeless zones and central heating began to oust coal fires.

Looking towards Oxford from Isis or Louse lock canal, 1920. The Oxford canal opened into a basin in New Road on 1 January 1790 and the lock in the foreground was added in 1796 to provide an improved link between the canal and the main River Thames away to the right. The Castle Mill Stream flows on towards Hythe Bridge past the site of the Cistercian Rewley Abbey, most of which was a coal yard at this time.

Isis lock today with trees obscuring distant views and the towpath a much narrower track for walkers and cyclists. Lord Nuffield bought the Oxford wharves in 1937 as the site for Nuffield College, and the surviving stub of the canal is now used for residential moorings. Trees to the right of the Castle Mill Stream now disguise housing on the site of the coal yard.

Osney lock, looking south towards the open spaces of Osney Mead, 1880s. River navigation around Oxford in the seventeenth and eighteenth centuries involved a circuitous journey along the Bulstake Stream. Prisoners from Oxford Castle were employed to build the first Osney lock at this point in 1790, giving boats a much more direct route along the course of the old Osney Abbey millstream.

Osney lock and the adjoining lock house were rebuilt in 1931. A large weir behind the danger sign cascades surplus water into a large pool and around the back of the lock. Trees in the background mask the Osney Mead industrial estate, which was created in the 1960s to provide space for local businesses that were housed in cramped or unsuitable accommodation.

A boy cools his feet in the river at the end of Marlborough Road, summer 1919. The houses opposite in Friars Wharf had replaced a substantial wharf of that name which had been quickly filled in and built over in the late 1840s as the Thames lost most of its commercial traffic to the railways.

A motor cruiser on the same stretch of river, viewed from the old gasworks pipe bridge that was converted into a footbridge in the 1970s. The houses on the opposite bank brought people back to St Ebbe's in the late 1970s and '80s after postwar slum clearance and planning blight had left much of the area empty. Trees and shrubs now give the once bleak Thames towpath on the right an almost rural appearance.

Folly Bridge from the west, *c*. 1880. The bridge took its name from Welcome's Folly, a former defensive gateway that was converted into a house in the seventeenth century. The folly, also known as Friar Bacon's Study, had been demolished in 1779 and the bridge itself was rebuilt in 1825–7. The stone building on the left was part of the city waterworks between 1826 and 1856, containing pumps which supplied untreated river water to the few consumers who had piped water.

The key features of this view are little changed, with the river flowing on beneath Folly Bridge and past the trees bordering Christ Church Meadow. The old waterworks, disused after 1856, became a council depot and housed the city's working horses until the 1930s. It was finally demolished along with adjoining houses in the early 1970s, and after the failure of a major hotel scheme Folly Bridge Court occupied the site in 1984.

Looking west from Abingdon Road at flood-time, *c.* 1868. Taunt took this photograph from the Grandpont or great bridge, originally constructed in the late eleventh century, which carries Abingdon Road across the Thames flood plain on some thirty-six arches. The distant railway truck was standing on the embankment of Oxford's first Great Western line, opened in 1844, which followed the course of the modern Marlborough Road down to the river.

Grandpont today with Waterman's Reach in the foreground; this development was built in the 1980s on the site of large wooden boathouses belonging to Salter Brothers. The Great Western moved its passenger station to Botley Road in 1852 and the goods station to Osney Lane in 1873. The company subsequently sold its Grandpont land, and house-building in the area began in the late 1870s.

Folly Bridge from the east, 1911. As rebuilt in the 1820s, Folly Bridge provided a basin for commercial river traffic beyond the three-arched bridge and navigation continued through a lock and under the single arch to the left of the picture. The lock was removed in the 1880s, and by this date Salter Brothers were running their boat-hiring business and river steamer service from the buildings in the foreground.

Salter's premises on Folly Bridge Island are little changed: the firm still hires out boats and takes passengers by steamer between Oxford and Abingdon on summer afternoons. The striking building on the left is the Hertford College Graduate Centre, designed by Oxford Architects Partnership and completed in 2000.

Iffley Mill, 1862. A mill on this site was first recorded in 1160 and these picturesque buildings must have been adapted and extended over many centuries. Many artists were drawn to the site and Henry Taunt, always keen to stress the artistic nature of his photographs, was quick to follow suit.

A narrowboat passes the weir and covered footbridge beside the site of Iffley Mill. The mill was gutted by fire on 27 May 1908 and never rebuilt. A plaque in Mill Lane commemorates the loss of this fine building.

Customers relaxing at the Swan Inn at Rose or Kennington Island, 1885. The ornate style of building must date from around 1840. By 1851 Kennington Island was a favourite resort attracting large numbers to Easter Monday entertainments despite an extremely wet afternoon. The pub was called the Swan by 1865 and it became the destination for many recreational outings from Oxford and Abingdon.

As more leisure opportunities became available in the twentieth century, fewer boating parties used the river and the Swan closed in 1926. The building is now a private house.

The King's Arms Hotel and the adjoining paper mill at Sandford-on-Thames, 1904. There was a watermill at Sandford by about 1170 and it was converted to paper-making in 1823; the mill had been extensively rebuilt after a fire in 1872. The King's Arms was first recorded in the later nineteenth century and the large advertising board in the garden indicates its popularity by the turn of the century.

Sandford paper mill closed in 1983 and riverside apartments soon occupied the site. No longer festooned with creeper, the King's Arms Hotel continues to flourish but most patrons today arrive by car and the riverside signboard has vanished.